Walk With Me

Through Stories of Faith

SYLVIA ENGEN ESPE

Walk With Me
Copyright © 2021 by Sylvia Engen Espe

Tellwell Talent
www.tellwell.ca

ISBN
978-0-2288-6010-5 (Hardcover)
978-0-2288-6009-9 (Paperback)
978-0-2288-6011-2 (eBook)

Table of Contents

Dedication

I dedicate this book to my family, extended family, relatives, and friends. I am appreciative to my family for encouraging me to write my memoirs. I trust each memory will prove to be a blessing to each one who reads these pages. Come, walk with me!

One

My Legacy

How do I begin to record as I reminisce the days of my life? How do I give priority to certain incidents, and perhaps forgo happenings that I should have remembered to include? My memories may differ from recollections others may remember from the past. I can only relate vivid memories that come quickly to my mind. I am now in my ninety third year of life; God has given me ninety three years of living on this earth. There have been highlights in my life that have brought me unspeakable joy. However, there have been moments of heart-wrenching sorrow that pierced to my innermost being. God, by His grace, carried me through such days.

I have been blessed with family, an extended family, relatives and friends who have upheld me, and supported me. I leave these life experiences, stressing God's goodness and grace in meeting these joys and sorrows, with you as a legacy from me. My family made our house a home, warmed my heart with their caring, listened to my woes, and forgiven me for the times I have regretted, be they regrettable words or deeds. I have made mistakes for which I am sorry. The beauty of character and display of affection of my family have touched my heart. Relatives have added joy to my life, grieved with me in times of sorrow, and inspired me to reach my desired goals. I have appreciated my friends who have listened to my concerns, supported my interests, and accepted me as I am.

I have limited my reminiscing to incidents that only involved my immediate family, including my parents. Come walk with me as I share these experiences with you.

11 Corinthians 1:3-4* states, "Praise be to the Lord Jesus Christ, the Father of compassion and the Father of all comfort, who comforts us in all our troubles, so that we can comfort those in any trouble with the comfort we ourselves have received from God."

Lord, may I be a blessing to others! Amen.
*NIV

Two

My Parent's First Child

"Your Dad and I were so pleased to have a baby of our own when you arrived," stated my Mother. "I told your Grandmother we had such a special baby. She only replied to me that even the mother crow thinks her babies are cute." But my mother assured me that she and Dad knew they were blessed with a gift from the Lord, as they did later after each of my siblings were born. Raising a first child with a mind of her own, I must admit, must have been a challenge. My Mother always boarded the teacher so I was aware of the school more than a mile from home. My Mother and Dad could not find their three-year-old one day. The hired man finally located me some distance from home on my way to "'chool." Mother washed clothes using a wash board in a tub of water. The soiled water, last used to wash the floor, sat outside on the porch. The hired man found me, clothes removed, enjoying a bath. Perhaps what bothered my Mother the most was to hear her brother saying that I should be spanked for biting his little daughter. I was not a model child.

However, I was blessed to have parents who treated me with grace, love, and forgiveness. Ephesians 6:1-4* states, "Children, obey your parents in the Lord, for this is right. 'Honour your father and mother' - which is the first commandment with a promise – that it may be go well with you and you may enjoy long life here on earth. Fathers, do not exasperate your children, instead, bring them up in the training and instruction of the Lord."It is our responsibility to honour our parents as long as we live.

Children are our heritage. May we always pray for our children as they grow from a child into adulthood, choose life professions, choose a life mate, and meet challenges and successes in their lives.

Lord, may we always obey You. Amen.
*NIV

Three

My First Vivid Memory

I was four years old. Prior intermittent memories before that age have crossed my mind but a vivid memory of a young girl upstairs in a Doctor's home remains with me. I remember the low ceiling above the table that was my bed. The Doctor had removed my tonsils. Perhaps the reason the picture in my mind is so clear was due to the pink ice cream cone my father brought to me. That cone was soothing to a sore throat. I thought it the best-tasting ice cream in the world.

Who is not happy eating an ice cream cone? Individuals from one year to a hundred years old enjoy ice-cream cones. My father could not have brought me a more appreciated gift. Luke 11:13* tells us, "If you then, though you are evil, know how to give good gifts to your children, how much more will your Father in heaven give the Holy Spirit to those who ask him." Our earthly fathers love their children. They are God's gift to them. They may make mistakes in life as all we humans do. However, all fathers wish the best for their dear children. We, as parents, are eager to protect our children at all times, regardless of demands made on us. My father met my need that day in the make-shift operating room upstairs in the Doctor's home. It began with the gift of love with a pink ice cream cone.

God designs us as parents to have generous hearts as we raise our children. Scripture tells us that parents are to treat their children well. But scripture reminds us that our heavenly Father has greater gifts for us than our earthly father can provide. The gift of the Holy Spirit is the most important gift. Jesus promised to give all believers this gift after His death, resurrection, and return to heaven. God is good.

Dear Lord, thank you for the love of my earthly father, and especially the love of my heavenly Father. Amen.
*NIV

Four

Childhood Memories

$\mathcal{I}$ remember tears trickling down my cheek after the school day was over. I was six years old. My Grade one teacher didn't wish to live alone in the room partitioned off in the corner of the school room. My parents agreed to have me live with her for the school week. They, I imagine, wanted to spare me the walk to school every day. My duty, after the closing bell rang, was to break twigs in the trees, a sufficient supply for heating mother's soup for our supper. It wasn't the broken branches that bruised my arms that brought the tears. I was homesick. I watched with envy as my school mates, carrying their lunch pails, merrily walked on their way home. There was no electricity so the creeping darkness of the large school room was frightening to me. My steps, as I walked across the school floor, creaked and groaned. The small cot, with wings to raise on either side, was the bed I shared with my teacher. I had a deep respect for her, but I feared I might touch her in the night. My homesickness increased at night fall. But I remember the joy of the morning. The bright sun shining through the huge windows transformed the schoolroom into a special day of learning. But I waited for Fridays when we could finally walk home.

Proverbs 3:20* tells us, "Children, obey your parents in everything, for this pleases the Lord." Proverbs 22:6* also states, "Train a child in the way he should go, and when he is old he will not turn away from it." Our parents wanted to make the best decisions for us as they knew best at the time. Is it not vital that parents seek God's guidance as they raise their children? Scripture states that it is God's will that we help our children understand, and believe God's promises in His Word throughout their lives.

Lord, thank you for parents, by example, who lived to glorify You. Amen.
*NIV

Five

Forgiven

"May I play in the old Model T?" was the request of each of our children every time we visited my parental home. "We pretend we travel all over the world in that car." This once shiny, black 1927 Model T had to have been Dad's pride and joy. It used to sit in the drive-through of the large granary. When I was around five years old, my younger brother and I put wheat in the radiator of the car. I am confident that it was my idea to "gas up" and then travel. Dad never did have the funds to repair the damage I had done to the car. The vehicle eventually was added to the area where discarded machinery met its resting place. Our family could no longer travel at forty miles an hour to church each Sunday. Dad had to face the cold winds of winter hanging on to the reins, guiding King and Berdie the five miles to church while mother and we children, wrapped in layers of clothes, sat huddled in the wagon. Blankets were placed on the horses while they were sheltered in the town Delivery Barn while we attended church service. Dad's Model T only achieved the rank of "Playhouse."

Pangs of guilt struck me each time I viewed the lonely and forlorn car in the machine graveyard. I am forever grateful to a father who never reminded me of the harm I had done to his beloved car. I do not remember any punishment. I only remember forgiveness from a loving father.

I am reminded of God's forgiveness when we ask Him to forgive us our sins. To forgive is to show love. There is healing and harmony when we forgive others. Love is the greatest gift we can give one another.

Isaiah 43:25* tells us, "I, even I, am he who blots out your transgressions, for my own sake, and remembers your sins no more."

Dear Lord, thank You for forgiving and forgetting our sins. Amen.
*NIV

Six

Forgive My Sin, Oh God.

"Children, come with me to the barn," requested my Dad one day many years ago. My brother and I followed our parent to the barn door that was on the ground being repaired. I was the oldest so I, no doubt, was the instigator of the fun we had in pounding nails into the door with our Dad's hammers. Our enjoyment we had of pretending we were carpenters with mighty weapons came to a halt when we saw our Dad come out to the barn to see what we were doing. I remember our Dad's words so clearly, "I can remove these nails from the door but each one will leave a hole in the barn door." He went on to say, "We cannot hide it when we do wrong."

The visible evidence of the holes in the barn door forever reminded me of my Dad's words each time I returned home to visit. Now the barn with the bruised door is no more, but the reminder of the lesson I learned as a small child lingers with me. I realize, as a Christian, that I have sinned in many ways. Sin always brings consequences. I realize that sin can come back to haunt me.

God sees our hearts. He knows the "holes" we have made on our lives journey. May we each ask God to forgive us for our sins of thought, word and deed. We know that God is ready to forgive us our sin as quickly as we ask Him to do so, but are we ready to forgive ourselves? He has told us that He forgives us our sins and then forgets them. May our lives be a reflection of God's great love for us. We are blessed.

Let us be reminded of Numbers 32b:23*, "You may be sure that your sin will find you out."

Dear Lord, thank you for parental guidance that taught us to obey Your Word each day of our lives. Amen.
*NIV

Seven

Obedience

"Yes, Mother, I am coming," I called back, "I will be there in a minute." But I didn't obey. I was absorbed in reading "Girl of the Limberlost." School library books fascinated me. The dish towel was often in one hand and my treasured book in the other. Books, The Young Cooperators in the Western Producer plus periodical reading material that came home with Dad's mail enticed me. The High School neighbour girl visited one day. She must have noticed that Mother was very busy but very tired. She tactfully scolded me for not helping my Mother as I should. She instructed me to get my chores completed before I read a book. I wasn't impressed but I needed her scolding.

Years went by and the time came for me to enter Nurses training. We Probies spent the first six months, not dressed in white, proudly working in a hospital, but in a classroom. Who was one of my teachers? The neighbour High School girl that taught me a needed lesson. She became my cherished mentor and my friend.

We read in Proverbs 1:8*, "Listen, my son, to your father's instructions and do not forsake your mother's teaching." We are to respect our parents. Leviticus 19:3* states, "Each of you must respect your mother and father... I am the Lord your God." Godly parents see the need to give advice to their children for their own good. We need to discipline ourselves to do whatever God's Word says to do or whatever the Holy Spirit speaks to our hearts to do. God offers us the grace to live a holy life that will bring blessings when we honour and obey Him by listening to His commands. We are to obey because we want to obey, not because "we have to." Then we are blessed!

To be obedient shows love for Jesus. John 14:15* tells us, "If you love me you will obey what I command."

Lord, thank you for parents who taught us to obey Your Word. Amen.
*NIV

Eight

God's Heaven

"Is it wrong of me to not want to go to heaven yet?" asked my Mother of our visiting Pastor. "I do not wish to leave my children when they are so young." I remember, as a preteen, standing by my Mother as the Pastor assured her that God knew how much her family needed her. It was the annual Bible Week in my home congregation. We, as young children, enjoyed the nightly trip to see our friends at church. My Mother was comforted by the Pastor's assurance that she had a ministry here on earth raising her family.

It was our Mother who made soup for a sick neighbour, baked bread for a lonely bachelor, and cleaned house for an elderly couple who lived in degrading conditions. It was our Mother who insisted, in retirement years, to care for chickens on the farm so "Something living was still needing my care." But moreover, Mother blessed us, her children, with her prayers for each one of us. We can thank God for the faithful Christian witness of our Mother who inspired us to live our lives for Christ.

Years have passed since my Mother questioned her own obedience to God's Word. She realized, as we do today, that His timing as to when He takes us to heaven is totally in His control. He has prepared the way for each one of us to obtain eternal life. God alone knows the rewards that will be ours when we enter the glorious streets of heaven.

"In my Father's house are many rooms; if it were not so, I would have told you. I am going there to prepare a place for you. And if I go and prepare a place for you, and I will come back and take you to be with me that you also may be where I am." John 14:2-3*

Dear Lord, thank you for God-fearing parents who instilled in us a longing to belong to you. Amen.
*NIV

Nine

Horses and Hay

"Get going Berdie and Queen," I called out loudly. "We are getting behind." I was doing my best as a young teenager to maneuver two horses. I sat proudly on my perch on the dump rake. The horses and I were raking the hay. Dad was ahead, directing Flory and King that were cutting the hay with a mower. As the wheels rotated forward on the dump rake, with its steel toothed claws, it lifted up, and dumped the load of hay into rows. Dad called these rows, "windrows." Dad picked up this hay manually with a fork, and piled it into a hay rack. The load had to be well balanced to guard against a tipping catastrophe. Hay was stored in the barn loft. Dad's livestock did not starve during winter months. This happened routinely years ago.

God blessed our childhood with horses for us to enjoy. They were part of our family; horses were vital to our way of life including Dad's farming, and our transportation. Horses are mentioned frequently in the Bible. They symbolized strength and endurance as well as human and worldly power.

But James 3:3* states, "When you put bits into the mouths of horses to make them obey us, we can turn the whole animal."

Isn't God telling us that our words can have control over a large horse, using the bit, a piece of metal attached to the bridle, to force the horse to turn in the direction we want it to go? We must not abuse the horse as our words are powerful. God has so completely met man's needs down through the ages; food for man and beast plus the availability of the means to obtain and use it. We, as the managers, must guard our words and motives as we control these God given gifts. Horses cutting hay and transporting it for storage was necessary for feeding livestock in winter. Horses made this possible!

Dear Lord, thank you for hay and thank you for horses! Amen.
*NIV

Ten

Living Trees

"It is time to cultivate our trees again," said Dad. It was my job to ride Bertie while Dad controlled the plow. I was the navigator; it wasn't always easy to steer my horse close enough to the rows of trees the Government had sent for our farm free of charge. Dad had worked diligently planting these five hundred spruce trees in our yard. I wasn't an avid horse rider but slow Bertie and I got along fine as he pulled the plow. It was Dad who sweat as he struggled with this machine. It was also the dear horse that worked hard. My sweat-coated pants were proof of that fact.

God has blessed our lives with the gift of trees. There are new buds emerging on the tree out my north window. A spruce tree is closer to the heavens as I look out to the west. The beauty of trees, which my Dad appreciated, enhanced the park-like setting of our home. Jeremiah 17:8b* tells us, "He will be like a tree planted in the water that sends out its roots by the stream. It does not fear when heat comes; its leaves are always green." Do you know that trees are mentioned frequently throughout the Bible from Genesis to Revelation?

We read in Genesis 2:9a*"And the Lord God made all kinds of trees grow out of the ground -

trees that were pleasing to the eye and good for food." God's gift of trees contributes to oil for dietary purposes, medical ingredients, beauty aids, and we good go on and on. But moreover, what would our landscape look like without trees? Every tree is different. Each tree adds to the beauty of the earth. Heavenly trees flourish because they are fed by heavenly water from above. We are also fed by the "heavenly" Word of God!

Dear Lord, thank you for the gift of trees that enhance our lives; shade for the weary, gives material needs, and adds to our lands beauty. Amen.
*NIV

Eleven

Anxiety

"The Veterinarian that tested our cows just phoned," Dad announced one day, "Molly has TB." I remember trembling with fear. This was frightening news to a fourteen year old farm girl. I had heard of a farmer's wife who had died of this disease. I prayed that no one in our family would become ill from drinking Molly's milk. But a vivid memory I have from years ago was the sudden realization that I might die. I remember wondering if I was good enough to go to heaven. I dared not ask my devout parents of my fear. They would expect me to know that I belonged to Jesus.

I have only two recollections of my first year attending Bible Camp that same summer. Our tent blew down in the middle of the night, and of a Pastor speaking on God's promise in John 3:16. He told us that a husband and wife promise their love for one another when they are married. The wife doesn't wake up each morning after their marriage and ask her husband if they are still married. "In the same way," the Pastor told us, "God has promised eternal life to all who believe on Him. We know. We do not go by our feelings!" I remember then claiming God's eternal life for me. I believed.

May we put our trust in God, believing that He gave His only Son to die on the cross to pay for our sins. We then can have the assurance that we have eternal life in His name. We will meet our loved ones in heaven some day.

Let us witness to others of the new life God bought for all of us who believe in Him as is promised in John 3:16*, "For God so loved the world that He gave His one and only Son, that whoever believes in Him shall have eternal life."

Dear Lord, we rejoice in your promise of eternal life for all of us who believe in You. Amen.
*NIV

Twelve

Go and Tell

"*D*o you know what I bought today?" asked Dad as he stepped down from his perch on the wagon seat, "I have a surprise for you." We waited patiently for Dad to put the horses in the barn. Dad brought a small package out of his pocket. "This is a crystal set." I remember the red box vibrated with music. We were shocked. Dad put a wind charger on top of our home several years later. He purchased ninety eight battery-like jars, and built shelves for them under the basement stair well. We could listen to a real radio when the wind blew. I remember Mother would often find the dish towel by the radio. We couldn't miss a program if it was a windy day. Our duties had to wait.

We are now living through a Pandemic. We are able to link with the world near and far through radio, TV, and electronic devises even though we are isolated in our own homes. I remember our Grandmother spoke of the isolation during the 1918 Spanish Flu. They had no way to communicate with one another. Mother spoke of going to many funerals where everyone wore masks.

I found a letter a neighbour, living one mile away, wrote to my Grandmother. We cannot fully identify with what our ancestors went through during those bleak years when deaths of the Great War, and the severe three waves of the Spanish Flu hit our world.

We are told that two billion people in this world have not heard about God's gospel. Matthew 28:19-20a* states, "Therefor go and make disciples of all nations, baptizing them in the name of the Father and the Holy Spirit, and teaching them to obey everything I have commanded you."

Does it not behoove us, who now have the means to communicate, to proclaim God's message of His death on the cross to pay for our sins to others throughout the world?

Lord, use me to communicate Your Word to all I meet. Amen.
*NIV

Thirteen

Sowing and Reaping

"The threshers are coming tomorrow," announced my Dad. "They will be here early in the morning." What excitement for we children! Mother had been busy making pies. Dad had prepared the barn for visiting horses. A large threshing machine was hauled to our field that evening. Early morning saw our quiet yard bustling with activity. The chug chug of the threshing equipment resounded through out the farm. I remember fearing threshers would fall off their high loads of sheaves in their hay racks as they approached the threshing machine. We waited for meal time. Mother brought her store of buns from the ice house. She prepared feasts for the hard working threshers for each meal. Our barn almost burst its seams with strange teams in each stall. I remember several of the threshers slept in the hay loft at night. Soon the workers, with their horses, were gone. The mighty threshing machine left Dad's fields. Our yard became quiet again. The high light of our late summer was over.

I thank God that I was born on a farm. My world was one of fascination for the opportunities nature gave me. The Bible states that the first job God gave man was to be a farmer. Do not farmers have a high calling from God? The earth, we read, belongs to the Lord.

Psalm 85:12* tell us,"The Lord will indeed give what is good, and our land will yield its harvest." Does it not behoove a farmer to be good steward of the land God has provided for him? John 4:34* states,"Do you not say, 'Four months more and then the harvest'"? I tell you, open your eyes and look at the fields! They are ripe for harvest." Doesn't Jesus compare the need to sow His message to others and pray for a harvest of believers to the role of a farmer who sows and then reaps his bounty?

Lord, may we be willing to sow your Word, and pray for a harvest of believers. Amen.
*NIV

Fourteen

Comfort and Coal

"Is Dad home yet?", asked Mother. We had stood by the east front room window for the past hour. Dad had left for the coal mines thirty miles away with King and Florey in the early morning hours. He went with lunch for himself, and food for the horses in the democrat wagon. We knew he dressed warmly, perched on the spring seat situated at the front of the wagon. It was time for Dad to get another load of coal. I remember Mother thanking God for Dad's safe return home, often in the late dark hours, each time he made these gruelling trips.

Coal is a solid and inflammable substance found underground. Lignite coal, burned in our home, was a fossil coal. It's volatile matter was expelled when exposed to a fire in the stove. It kept red heat for some time. My Grandmother stayed up late each evening in order to put a large chunk of coal in the stove that would keep the house warm until morning. Opening the oven door offered warmth. Ashes frequently required disposal, but aided in getting Dad's car to start easily when put under the vehicle's motor. No one complained of the clinkers, or the dirty, greasy coal pail that frequently needed replenishing. Coal was also used to power locomotives, steam driven mills, and steam engines. It has now been replaced by natural gas, solar and wind power.

The Bible speaks of "hot coals" frequently as in Proverbs 6:28a,* "Can a man walk on hot coals with out his feet becoming scorched?" The heat of hot coals was recognized to be a source of warmth.

We are admonished in James 2:16,* "If one of you says to him, 'Go, I wish you well, keep warm and well fed,' but does nothing about his physical needs, what good is it?" Use us, Lord, as coal did for us, to bring your warmth and comfort to others.

Lord, thank you for giving us parents that supplied all our needs. Amen.
*NIV

Fifteen

Sunday School at Home

"It is time for Sunday School," Mother would tell us on Sunday mornings. I remember we children would scamper to the brown couch, a "Sunday pew," for our "church-at-home" lesson. Mother sat facing us, relating Bible stories that captivated our attention. Mother brought scripture alive for us. She role modelled love and faith in God for her family. Travelling miles with horses in blustery winter weather in order to get to church was not as comfortable as being seated next to the coal heater in the comfort of our living room. Church was the centre of our social life when the weather cooperated, and transportation was available. My parents taught us that God is everywhere, even on our farm. Walking with our family along the country road, or sitting in the shade of the red barn gave us each the opportunity to feel God's presence. I remember not being able to find the cows one day when I was on my daily chore of bringing home the cows for evening milking. I remember asking God to help me find them. I promptly saw the location of the cows. I was overjoyed. God heard me as I walked among gophers in the west pasture.

"Give me a child until he is seven and then you can have him," a local priest told my Dad years ago. Should not our memories of our homes be of a God-centred-church home where God is glorified in all daily life activities? Let us use every opportunity to teach our children about God's love as Moses instructed, "Love the Lord with all your heart and with all your soul and with all your strength. These commandments I give you today are to be upon your hearts. Talk about them when you sit at home and when you walk along the road, when you lie down and when you get up." Deuteronomy 6:5-7*

Dear Lord, may our children grow up to live for you everyday of their lives. Amen.
*NIV

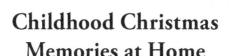

Sixteen

Childhood Christmas Memories at Home

"*D*ad is almost home," I called from my perch at the upstairs window, "I can see the wagon and horses coming through the gate." It was just two days before Christmas Eve. It wasn't easy to wait for the parcel from Eaton's Christmas Wish catalogue to arrive. Threaded popcorn was ready to be put on the Christmas tree Dad would bring home from town. Little Christmas Eve, December 23rd, as Grandma called it, finally arrived. This was the day the Christmas tree came to life in the front room. Gifts were wrapped and decorations brightened our home. How we waited for Christmas Eve to arrive. It was a highlight of the season. Mother's lutefiske supper which included lefsa, and a Julekake, a bun shaped fruit bread left on each plate, was a meal we keenly enjoyed. We had difficulty waiting to move into the front room where the gifts were under the tree. Dad read about the birth of Jesus found in the second chapter of Luke. He threatened at times to read on and on, knowing how impatient we were to receive our gifts. A short program often followed. Receiving our gifts brought joy and much happiness. Christmas morning found us at church followed by dinner with our Grandma who served the best potato lefsa.

What child doesn't wait for Christmas? No matter what happens in life, Jesus is the light that came to us at Christmas regardless of the darkness of the world. Christmas is the time to remember Jesus birth, and the time to thank God for His amazing and enduring gift of hope. The account of Jesus's birth has inspired many to compose carols that live on throughout the years. Luke 2:14* tells us, "Glory to God in the highest, and on earth peace to men on whom His favour rest."

Dear Lord, thank you for the gift of the Christ Child, and the keen anticipation of it when a child, and making it new each year as we age. Amen.
*NIV

Seventeen

Childhood Christmas Memories at School

"*H*urry, it is time to leave for the Christmas Concert," called my mother, "Dad is waiting for us in the car." The day had finally arrived. Practising for the concert was a happy change from working with fractions and learning about the First World War. Drills required fun rehearsals. Christmas carols resounded throughout the school room, and recitations were repeated over and over. Our mothers did their part by lending bed sheets that were used for stage curtains. Our fathers brought boards for seating. Mothers brought the brown bags that had been filled with oranges, Christmas candies, and popcorn. Several fathers brought gas lamps that lit up the large school room. Our parents sat proudly while we performed, dressed in our very best. Excitement was in the air. We didn't notice the sound of creaks and groans as we took each step on the school floor boards. The light of the gas lamps clothed the room into a magical concert hall. The school entry floor was filled with overshoes and boots of all sizes. We all went home proudly carrying a brown bag of goodies. The magical night was over.

Each School Christmas concert was special in the fact that time was given to share with all that Jesus's birth was the reason for us to celebrate. We were told the most important event in history happened when Jesus was born in a manger in Bethlehem. The Jews had waited for year s and years for the promised Messiah to be born. He came into the world in a humble stable. "Today in the town of David, a Savior has been born to you; he is Christ the Lord." Luke 2:11*. We were reminded that Jesus is the source of life; reminded that God speaks to us through His Word, and also through believers that live in our midst. We are blessed.

Dear Lord, thank you for the gift of the Christ Child that came into the world to die for our sins. Amen.
*NIV

Eighteen

Childhood Christmas
Memories at Church

"The Sunday School Concert," reminded mother one morning, "is today." This was a highlight for we children. We had practised faithfully in preparation for a festive evening to celebrate the birth of our Lord. The angels, wise men, shepherds, Joseph, Mary, and baby Jesus, all dressed in appropriate costumes, vividly presented the events that took place years ago in Bethlehem. Christmas carols were sung enthusiastically. A Christmas tree at the front of the church sat proudly. It boasted gleaming candles that illuminated the sanctuary. A pail of water sat behind the tree, in readiness in case of a feared fire. Church services held during the Christmas season created an atmosphere of hope and fulfillment as we praised God for the gift of His Son who was born in Bethlehem. He came to die on the cross to pay for our sins. Thank you, Jesus.

A birth announcement found in Luke 2:8-10* tells us, "And there were shepherds living out in the fields nearby, keeping watch over their flocks at night. An angel of the Lord appeared to them, and the glory of the Lord shone around them, and they were terrified. But the angel said to them, "Do not be afraid, I bring you good news of great joy that will be for all people." The shepherds were the first to see baby Jesus. They spread the good news of Jesus's birth to others. The Israelis had waited for years and years for the birth of the Messiah. It is heart warming to learn that the humble shepherds were the first people to be told the good news. Jesus comes to everyone who is humble; has a humble heart to accept Him into their lives. Christmas carols remind us each year of Christ coming to earth to die on the cross for us. You alone give us peace. Thank you, Lord.

Dear Lord, may we be just as eager as the shepherds to tell others of your blessings that you bestow on us. Amen.
*NIV

The Homestead

I was intrigued with Grandma's Sunday-company pillow cases. An embroidered message immaculately stitched with satin thread read, "I slept and found life was beauty. I awakened and found life was duty." This courageous lady faced many hours of being "dutiful" on a primitive homestead.

A sod house, where the only place to keep the flour sack dry was under the kitchen table, failed to keep the family warm on cold, bitter nights. Food was sparse until untamed soil was prepared for a garden and grain crop. Grandma spoke of mosquitoes, threatening wild fires, and extreme heat that was difficult to endure. But her faith and fortitude led her to see a school district formed. The first Ladies Aid met in her home. The sale of their handiwork, $200.00, paid for a pastor. She did her part in helping to form a God centred community.

This homestead became my home. Dad took over the farm at a young age. Grandma left the farm she helped to shape when my parents were married, This was the farm where I was born. It was Grandma's school with a treasured library that hooked my imagination. I worked in flower beds where Grandma, no doubt, had formed with her shovel and determination. I milked cows in the barn where a cow had stamped on my Grandma's foot, leaving her with an injury that caused her life-long pain. This farm remained in our family for over a century.

I found Revelation 2:10* written in Grandma's handwriting on the back page of her worn Bible, "Be faithful, even to the point of death, and I will give you the crown of life."

May we thank God for God fearing pioneers who withstood a difficult life that included hardships and calamities in order to form a community that we are blessed to inherit. This is the legacy they have left us. Are we doing our part to ensure that our community remains a Christ centred community?

Lord, thank you for God fearing pioneers.
Amen.
*NIV

Twenty

Mother

"Here we are, Mom," we children announced as we reached home after school. It was wash day. Mother was still scrubbing clothes on the washboard. Our job, once we had enjoyed chokecherry syrup on bread, was to pour the wash water on Mother's flower beds. There were more clothes to hang on the clothes line. I had to bring the cows home. Mother had to start making supper. The teacher who occupied our west bedroom upstairs would soon be home. Dad would come in from the field. There were days Mother helped with milking when Dad had to work late. Eggs had to be collected, and chickens fed. Pigs required food if Dad was late in getting home. Mother's work was never done.

"Her children arise and call her blessed; her husband also, and he praises her," states Proverbs 31:28.* This verse described our Mother. Home was a safe place, and a loving place because Mother was there. It was Mother who nourished us as babies, and comforted us in her arms. It was Mother who made delicious home made bread, sewed new dresses for us each Christmas, and made ice cream in a pail that swayed on the clothes line on cold, windy days. Our Roger's Syrup lunch pail often contained a surprise we enjoyed at our noon lunch at school. Mother reflected God's character each day.

Isn't a godly mother the highest calling of womanhood? What Mother taught us when we were young is planted in our hearts.

Our Mother's devout Christian influence in our family, and her faithful attention to all our needs could be compared to the love and care our heavenly Father bestows on us.

We are His children. Being a part of a loving family teaches us how much God loves us. 1 John 4:19* states "We love because he first loved us." God's love is the source of all love. May we all honour our Mothers with love.

Dear Lord, thank you for my Christian Mother and for all godly Mothers. Amen.
*NIV

Twenty One

Home

"It's time to go out to the field, children," said our Dad, "Time to go stooking." Dad drove the horses that pulled the binder around the field. The binder, periodically, spewed out bundle after bundle of cut grain stalks on the ground in readiness for stooking. A stook is an arrangement of theses sheaves or bundles into a shape of a teepee. We had to make two bundles stand up by facing each other, place a bundle on either side, and flank four more bundles around the middle sheaves. The stook kept the grain heads off the ground, aided the grain to dry, and helped shed the rain. However, the highlight of this labour was sharing cookies, apples and water that Mom packed for us. We marked our first stook with additional bundles so it was easily identified. It was "King of our Stooks," our home base that we ran to many times because we placed Mom's goodies inside of it. It gave us a sense of feeling grounded in a field filled with bundles waiting for our attention. This stook was a haven for two hard working farm children who sat in its shade as we enjoyed our lunch.

We all need a home base here on earth. Christ should be the foundation of the framework of our home so we feel safe and happy. Our home should give us a sense of feeling grounded just at the "King Stook" was special to us out in the grain field. However, we are blessed to know God has promised us a home in heaven that cannot be compared to our home here on earth. We can not, with our limited understanding, fathom the wonders of heaven above. God is good! Let us listen to what God tells us in 1 Corinthians 2:9*, "No eye hath seen, nor ear has heard, no mind has conceived what God has prepared for those who love him."

Dear Lord, thank you for promising a heavenly home for all who believe in You. Amen.

*NIV

Twenty Two

Contentment

"Great! Mother is finished," I happily explained, "she has put new straw in our mattress." This was a yearly task for our Mother each fall during the depression. Old straw was removed, and father brought fine golden straw from the thrashing machine in sufficient quantity to replenish the sagging mattresses. There wasn't money to purchase regular mattresses. We children were thrilled to sleep on new hills and in valleys. We rolled around until our mattress took on our body form. We could then nestle in a nest that gave us comfort and contentment. This was luxury to us. We were happy for small improvements of any kind.

We read in Philippians 4: 11-13*,"I am not saying this because I am in need, for I have learned to be content whatever the circumstances. I know what it is to be in need, and I know what it is to have plenty. I have learned the secret of being content in any and every situation, whether well fed or hungry, whether living in plenty or in want. I can do everything in him who gives the strength." We can only find contentment in Christ. God is sufficient to meet every need. We can be content in every circumstance when we know God, and delight in His goodness to us. God will supply our needs in a way that He knows what is best for us.

Are you discontent because you do not have what you want? Do you look to the world to satisfy the void in your life? Only Christ can fulfill that void. God's love embraces us which brings satisfaction regardless of our circumstances. 1 Timothy 6:6-8,* states, "But Godliness with contentment is great gain. We brought nothing into the world and we take nothing out of it. But if we have food and clothing, we will be content." May we find contentment in Christ.

Dear Lord, take away our desires to want what is not good for us. Help us to be content in every circumstance. Amen.
*NIV

Twenty Three

Scarlet Fever

I was thirteen years old when I was diagnosed with Scarlet Fever, a contagious bacterial infection that affects children from ages five to fifteen. I know that I was quite ill with a high fever and severe sore throat. I marvel today to realize that my Mother had to have practised excellent isolation techniques. I am not aware of anyone who contracted this disease from me. I do remember our family was quarantined. I have faint recollections of the doctor coming to our home to help Mother fumigate the house. Incense-like cones were placed on each step of the staircase. I remember a strange odor spread throughout the house as a result. We had to vacate our home for a day. I was later fitted for glasses, and I became allergic to a drug that was given me throughout the illness.

My Mother has to be commended for the nursing care she gave me. She wanted to become a nurse. Such training was not available in her region. We read in Isaiah 66:13-14a*, "As a mother comforts her child, so will I comfort you; and you will be comforted over Jerusalem. When you see this, your heart will rejoice and you will flourish like grass; the hand of the Lord will be made known to his servants." Our mother's love is modelled by our Savior. Psalm

107:20-21b tells us, "He sent forth his word and healed them: he rescued them from the grave. Let them give thanks to the lord for his unfailing love and his wonderful deeds for men. Let them sacrifice thank offerings and tell of his works with words of joy."

May we bring our ill children to God in prayer, believing that He will answer our prayers We cannot say, "All I can do is pray." when our children are ill. Bringing such requests to God should be our first step. Our heavenly Father waits to hear from us.

Dear Lord, thank you for caring for us in sickness and in heath. Amen.
*NIV

Twenty Four

New Life

"I must have chickens, "my Mother firmly stated. "I still want some thing living on on our farm!" Aged parents were giving up many of the activities that had kept them toiling day after day on our homestead. However, a farm with new life as baby chicks to keep the yard alive was of vital importance to my Mother. She would mash boiled eggs for a treat for her little creatures.

Chickens played a great role during my childhood. They contributed meat and eggs to Mother's table feasts. It was the eggs that paid much of the grocery bill. I remember, as a new teenager, hauling a double apple box up to the barn loft. I found two clucking hens and gave them each a nest of eggs. I put up temporary bars to keep them from fleeing, only to find out that the bars were not required. Daily feedings of food and water kept me occupied after school. The arrival of baby chicks was a highlight that I will always remember.

Eggs are traditionally a symbol of new life. We associate baby chicks with new beginnings. Spring, when there is new growth, reveals new life. The farmer cultivates the soil, the seed he plants sprouts, and there are green fields. The Bible tells us Jesus was given new life after He died on the cross for our sins. He rose up to be with God. We, too, are given new life when we become a child of God. Our heavenly Father has promised to care for us, His children, just as a mother hen cares for her brood. Luke 13:34b* states, "How often I have longed to gather your children together, as a hen gathers her chicks under her wings, but you were not willing." Mother hens have been known to die in a fire, leaving their chicks untouched because they were safe under their mother's wings. Even so Jesus protects us!

Dear Lord, thank you for the new life we have as your child. Amen.
*NIV

Twenty Five

I'm Learning, Lord.

"*Y*ou may go on the floor next week," stated my Supervisor. "You will have your first patient of your own." I was elated. Nurses training, the last while, was spent in the Service Room, cleaning and shining stainless steel equipment. This experience without any glory, was not part of my dreams to some day become a nurse. I was in awe of being able to help someone who needed my assistance.

Morning care proceeded uneventfully with a quiet, sullen patient. My efforts to encourage comfortable conversation didn't ensue. I wanted to witness of my faith in the Lord so I, trembling with nervousness, bluntly asked her, "Are you a Christian?"

My startled patient turned abruptly towards me, stating emphatically, "Well I should hope so!" I stepped back, wordless and humbled. I realized I had lessons to learn if I could be an effective witness for Christ.

Webster defines "witness"- to tell of the truth and genuineness of something." I soon realized it is simply sharing with others what Christ personally means to me. Jesus was crucified on the cross to pay for my sins. I want to tell others of the peace and joy that I have in Him. I realized my faith is reflected in my conduct in all circumstances. The lesson I learned years ago caring for my first patient taught me I needed to delicately, lovingly, and tactfully witness to others of God's love that led Him to pay for the sins of all, including me.

May this be our prayer, "Pray for me, that whenever I open my mouth, words may be given to me that I will fearlessly make known the mystery of the gospel, for which I am an ambassador in chains. Pray that I will declare it fearlessly as I should" Ephesians 6:19-20*.

Dear Lord, forgive us for the times we have failed to witness of your love that led you to die on the cross to pay for our sins. Amen.
*NIV

Twenty Six

The Polio Virus

The year was 1952. I was nursing in a hospital thirty miles from home. I was taking care of Polio patients. Polio is an infectious, disabling, and life-threatening disease caused by the polio virus. It infects the spinal cord so causes paralysis. Our Polio unit included an iron lung, a large tank respirator that pulled air in and out of the lungs so the patient could breathe. Excellent isolation technique gave me assurance and confidence. My patients were adults. They understood why they had pain and discomfort. Innocent little children did not.

However, an aunt of the family I lived with became upset when she learned that a nurse living with her nieces and nephews, was working in a Polio unit. I understood her concern, but it did cause me uneasiness. This most feared disease also caused concern to everyone in the city. In fact, it was the most dreaded disease in the 1940s and early 1950s. President Roosevelt, a Polio victim, organized the March of Dimes which supported 1.8 million school children involved in the largest medical study in history. The world rejoiced when Dr. Salk's vaccine almost eradicated Polio in 1955. Smallpox was the only disease eradicated by a vaccine prior to this time. Vaccines have saved millions of lives. I believe the discovery of vaccines has been God's miracle gift in helping to eradicate various illnesses. God has given keen minds the knowledge and expertise to create effective vaccines. Our city, a concerned aunt, and I breathed a prayer of thanks when the Polio epidemic was over.

Jesus has promised to be with us during times of sickness and distress. Matthew 4:23-24a* reads, "Jesus went throughout the Galilee, teaching in their synagogues, teaching the good news of the kingdom, and healing every disease and sickness among the people. News about him spread all over Syria, and people brought to him all who were ill with various diseases." God heals today.

Dear Lord, thanks for giving mankind the skills to make effective vaccines! Amen.
*NIV

Twenty Seven

Fulfillment

"Some day I would like a muskrat coat," I told my Mother. "Do you think that will ever happen?" I was a teenager with fascinating dreams. Nurses training provided me with a monthly six dollar check. My first payment after graduating and one month employment was meagre in comparison to day's wages, but it was gold in my hands. Strolling through stores with money that I had earned in my pocket put me in high spirits. I found, to my surprise, a muskrat coat sale. I walked to my residence with a new coat, and a contract promising a monthly payment of twenty-five dollars. Those payments crippled my expenses greatly. I was satisfying my own desires, and I paid for it.

Despite the financial hardship it cost me, the muskrat coat lived on. The hem of the coat wore from too much contact with my high boots. The top of the car seat wore the fur of the upper back portion of the coat. I made a new three quarter length coat which served me well. Cutting it up with scissors, I found out later, was a mistake. My husband and I fought fur in our home, and I am afraid, ate fur for over a month. The coat's last years were spent with my Mother. She wore it in winter when she fed her chickens.

We read in Psalm 20:4* "May he give you the desires of your heart and make all your plans succeed." Psalm 20:5b* states * "May the Lord grant all your requests." My yearning for a muskrat coat came from a vain desire on my part. But I realize the many years that it was used in my life saved the expense of purchasing another coat. My pastor husband's wages were not sufficient for such added expenses. We have a heavenly Father who, in His wisdom, hears our prayer requests, and answers them according to His will.

Dear Lord, thank you for your care for us, and for supplying all our needs. Amen.
*NIV

Twenty Eight

SLBI

"**M**om, did you really coach Girl's Basket ball?" skeptically asked my son. I had to reply that I did when young and yearned for a challenge. I was on staff at Saskatchewan Lutheran Bible Institute. I had to admit to him that coaching Soft ball was much easier. Touching the lives of young students invigorated me. Their enthusiasm was contagious. Student's problems were varied, but sharing them brought a closer relationship between the student and acting councillor. My days were full but satisfying.

Hockey was a popular sport at the school. The Seminary hockey team arrived one day in May. One of the Defence men asked for the nurse. He had a headache. That was the beginning of a romance that led to a happy marriage almost two years later.

Scripture tells us in Psalm 37:4-6*,"Delight yourself in the LORD and he will give you the desires of your heart. Commit your way to the LORD; trust in him and he will do this: He will make your righteousness shine like the dawn, the justice of your cause like the noon day sun." God does give us the desires of our heart according to His will. The more we seek God, the more we are blessed as we draw closer to Him. God asks us to live for

Him; to make Him the centre of our lives. Doesn't it behoove us to spend more time in prayer as well as more time in reading His Word? We must know the Lord better, and delight in His presence. We will then, as we walk with Him, know true joy.

Psalm 37:7a* goes on to say, "Be still before the Lord and wait patiently for Him." God's timing isn't always our timing. We should be willing to wait patiently for God to work out His plans for us. May we entrust ourselves completely to the Lord's control and guidance. We will be rewarded.

Dear Lord, thank you for giving us the desires of our hearts according to Your will. Amen.
*NIV

Our First Home

"I am frightened," I frantically told my husband as we approached turbulent waves. "I do not see a ferry." We stopped at the edge of rushing water, hardly distinguishable in the impending darkness. The second hand-ringer washer, filled with wedding gifts, jolted in the back seat. Finally, a dark, looming watercraft noisily approached us. I breathed a prayer of thanks when we actually reached the far side of the river safely. We were on our way to my husband's first parish in the northern area of the province. The warm welcome of the parishioners touched our hearts. We felt welcomed and blessed beyond expectation. But living accommodations required acceptance on our part; we learned from that experience. We didn't have running water. We fetched it from a well. Due to the hardness of the water, snow had to be melted in the barrel by the stove for washing clothes. We had no fridge so the cream sat in an orange box lowered into the well. There was one condemned plugin. An apple box with a towel rack sufficed for a sink. I tried to can fruit as we didn't have a deep freeze. Three jars exploded.

We spent days periodically cutting logs in the wooded areas for fuel. A farmer left a cream can of skimmed milk on our door step periodically. A wedding gift-a mix master-faithfully churned our gifts of cream into butter. Despite the learning curves we experienced, life in the new parish was filled with love and kindness. We had electricity and a cistern before the year was over. I learned to cook the hard way as I served workers their meals while they made our home improvements.

I am reminded of Romans 15:7*, "Accept one another, then, just as Christ accepted you, in order to bring praise to God." We were accepted. When Jesus lived on earth, He welcomed and blessed all people. Dare we exclude others?

Lord, may we follow God's welcome attitude in our home and into our Church. Amen.
*NIV

Thirty

The Red Book

"We do not seem to live very long in our family," my fiance casually told me one day. Several in my family have passed away from heart problems." I gave little thought to this health history. We were both young and well so why shouldn't we both enjoy good health for many years to come? We rejoiced in our mutual love. Marriage brought fulfillment to our dreams. Each day was a delight. However, a book entitled, "Heart Attack, are You a Candidate?" sat on our bookshelf. We never touched this red hard cover book that sat like a threatening bomb. But there were days and nights when the thought of loosing a loving husband and father filled me with fear. I was haunted periodically by the knowledge of health problems in my husbands family. How could I ever cope without him at my side?

The day did come when I had to say an earthly good bye to the love of my life. I felt like half of me was missing. "Dear God," I prayed, "How can I cope without my soulmate, my confidant, and my best friend?" God slowly answered my prayer. His presence wrapped me in a cloak of comfort and peace. There were difficult days but God did not forsake me. I regret the fact that I spent hours of our married life threatened by the red book on our bookshelf. I missed days when I could have rejoiced every moment with my family instead of fearing the day when father would not be with us.

God asks us to rejoice and be glad each day that He has given us. God has not promised us that life would always be easy. We all face problems and challenges. Each day is a gift. "This is the day the Lord has made; let us rejoice and be glad in it." Psalm 118:24*.

Lord, thank you for promising that you will never forsake us as we meet challenges in our lives. Amen.
*NIV

Thirty One

My Error

*W*hy do memories, especially when embarrassment is involved, linger with me years later? We had just moved to a new parish. We were strangers in an unfamiliar town. My husband was asked to conduct a funeral two days after we arrived. I realized that we were low on groceries that morning. I ventured out on the driveway aiming to find the grocery store I had noticed when we drove into town. I was surprised to see the amount of traffic on our street. I took my chance to get on my way when there was a brief break in traffic. "Someone does it every time,"exclaimed the funeral director to my husband seated beside him in the hearse. "It never fails, you would think people would realize that this is a funeral procession." My embarrassed husband never dared let on that the intruder was his wife behind the wheel.

I was soon to realize the role of a pastor's wife was a learning experience. I was thankful for a forgiving husband who put up with the blunders I made. He taught me that Parishioners spoke to him in confidence. He could not share them with his wife. I learned that we could not have special friends. We tried our best to treat everyone alike. But Parishioners treated us like royalty.

Scripture tells us it is more blessed to give than to receive. Gifts of food frequently came to our door. There were times we received a product that our garden had already yielded in abundance. We thankfully received them knowing the givers were blessed in sharing their gifts. We lived and served people we learned to love. We left part of our hearts behind each time we parted from a congregation. "Then I will give you shepherds after my own heart, who will lead you with knowledge and understanding," Jeremiah 3:15*. Pastoral care is not about us, but about serving our Lord.

Dear Lord, thank you for accepting us to be servant leaders for you. Amen.
*NIV

Thirty Two

Our First Born

"It is true," I happily told my husband, "We are going to be parents." The excitement of the prospects to have a family of our own brought us a sense of keen jubilation. There had not been a baby in the parsonage for over forty years. Coffee was no longer my friend. My husband drank his coffee plus mine when we attended functions as the local Ladies Aid. We wanted to keep our secret. However, in less than two months, I was ordered to be on bed rest due to elevated blood pressure. This was difficult for a young wife who rarely was ill. Nurses training taught me that five percent of first pregnancies became toxic. I was in that group. My husband had to leave food at my bedside Sunday mornings as he travelled over a hundred miles conducting services in three different churches. Toxemia kept me in bed for over seven months.

"Am I a father yet?" my husband called while conducting a service forty miles away. The Nurse told me later that she didn't dare tell him that he had a daughter as they had not been able to get any response from our baby. There were only hot and cold tubs used for resuscitation in the hospital. I was heavily sedated due to complications of Toxemia. By the time the new Dad arrived, our baby girl had responded, and I was aware of my surroundings. We were blessed with three more children to complete our family. Toxemia was not a factor again. God was with us. We were blessed.

"I prayed for this child, and the Lord has granted me what I have asked of Him." is found in 1 Samuel 1:27*. There are many Bible verses that stress God's value of little people. They are a reward from the Lord. We prayed for God's wisdom and guidance as they grew into adulthood.

Dear Lord, thank you for the gift of children you gave to us to love and cherish. Amen.
*NIV

Thirty Three

You Hold Me in Your Hand

I hesitate each time I step on a descending escalator. My heart beats faster, and my feet immovable. Our three year old daughter, years ago, looked with amazement at moving stairs in a city department store. This was a new sight for a young girl from a small town. She was fascinated with the expectation of riding on steps that would actually move.

I remember clutching my daughter's hand as we hesitantly stepped on to the rushing escalator. Suddenly, a teenager bounded down the steps passed us, oblivious to the girl he pushed off balance. God strengthened my right hand, strengthened the grip that kept our child at my side. Steel bars with protruding ridges loomed before me. Those protrusions could have permanently injured our daughter. That frightening vision remains with me to this day.

My heart filled with gratitude to God who saved our little girl from harm. God gave me sufficient strength to keep her balanced. I was reminded that our Heavenly Father holds us in His grip when we lose our balance. We have the assurance that Our Saviour is always present to protect us – in the Hudson Bay Store in the city or in our Safeway Store at home.

Though our strength may fail, we can be assured that God is with us to protect us. He holds our right hand whether we be young or old. God has us in His grip from birth to death. We are blessed.

Psalm 71:4* states "Deliver me, O my God, from the hand of the wicked, from the grasp of evil and cruel men." Then remember God's promise in Psalm 73:23* "Yet I am with you; you hold me in your hand."

Dear Lord, thank you for holding us in Your grip. Thank you for the comfort we find in Your assurance that you always will hold our hand on our journey through life. Amen.
*NIV

Thirty Four

Loyalty

"May we have a dog?" asked one of our children when we moved to a parsonage in the country. "We do want a dog," echoed the rest of the family. A black pup soon became part of our family. Lad faithfully followed our two year old, seemingly knowing that the two of them were in the "learning to be independent" stages of life. Lad would force himself between my daughter and myself if I ever had to correct her. Lad never slept in the heated garage. He slept against our front door, despite extreme cold nights, closer to the girl he worshipped. Time came for us to move from the country setting to a city. Lad saw us bring suit cases to the car. He made his way to the floor in front of the back seat. We spent some time coaxing him to get out of the car. He didn't budge. Big brother had to carry the heavy dog away from his fortified place. We knew Lad could never adjust to living in a city. A neighbouring farmer asked to have Lad. We were notified two weeks later that Lad was found diseased. We speculated of his cause of death. "Did Lad die from a broken heart?"

To be loyal, Webster's dictionary tells us, is "to be faithful and steadfast." We are blessed if we have a truly loyal friend who accepts us just as we are. Such a friend is a treasure. Scripture tells us of Ruth's loyalty to her mother-in-law in Ruth1:16*, "Don't urge me to leave you or to turn back from you. Where you go I will go, and where you stay I will stay. Your people will be my people, and your God, my God."

But we cannot compare Lad's loyalty nor the loyalty of any human being to the loyalty God reveals to us. He died for us, loves us and forgives us. His loyalty never ends.

Lord, may we constantly be loyal to You. Be first in our lives! Amen.
*NIV

Thirty Five

Teach Me!

"This was my worst day of school," our eight-year-old daughter exclaimed when when she came home. "I told them I was related to Grannie on the Hillbillies, and no one would believe me." Grannie's sister married a distant relative in Missouri. She continued, "They only laughed at me." The "Show and Tell" period proved to be devastating for the young girl.

However my daughter has much to teach me. She never holds a grudge. She has met various challenges in life that I doubt I could have withstood so forgivingly. She lives each day with a ready smile. I am sure we all have met situations where we momentarily have felt slighted. Life is not without difficulties. But how do we react to them? The pain of a personal grudge is agonizing to take. Holding on to that pain makes it more difficult to endure. God asks us to forgive in all situations. Putting up with a chronic disease could cause many to feel the diagnosis is another reason to hold a grudge, and thus be filled with stress and bitterness. She does not complain. My daughter takes it in her stride. Ephesians 4:23-24 and 32* tell us, "Put on the new attitudes of your minds: and put on the new self, created to be like God in true righteousness and holiness... Be kind and compassionate to one another, forgiving one and other, but as in Christ God forgave you."

Our willingness to love and forgive in all situations is visible in our actions and conduct. We can then have inner peace. Do we not live as children of light when we listen to God? Does not our former negative attitude take wings on a positive outlook that lead us up Christ-directed paths? May we act in love, and with a smile each day that we live. Be we slighted or not, may we live for You, dear Lord!

Dear God, thank you for acting in love when you sent your Son to die for our sins. Amen.

*NIV

Thirty Six

Determination

"I want to go to town to night," demanded our six year old daughter. She had spent a day with her friend at a Vacation Bible School earlier in the week. "They are having a program at their church tonight, and I want to be there." Our country parsonage was eight miles away. I was unable to fulfill her desires. She had just attended her own VBS program held in our church the week before. Time went by. I was suddenly aware of our daughter's absence. Calling her brought no response. I desperately searched our home. I failed to see her down our lane. I finally decided to take our car in an attempt to find her. I had travelled some distance before I spied a little girl, dressed in her Sunday best, walking at top speed, less than one mile from her eight mile destination. That was our girl. Her determination led her down challenging paths that have proved to bring benefits in life beyond her expectations.

I have frequently asked myself, "Have I consistently directed my children in the right direction when they have sought my reactions to decisions that they are contemplating? Have I asked God to lead me as I fill the mother role in our home? 11 Timothy 3:14-15* reads, "As for you, continue in what you have learned and have become convinced of, because you know from whom you have learned it, and how from infancy you have known the holy scriptures, which are able to make you wise for salvation through faith in Christ Jesus."

It is our prayer that our children do not stray from the truths they were taught as child. May we, as Timothy's grandmother Lois, and his mother Eunice, in 11 Timothy 1:5*, ensure our children learn of Jesus's deep love for them that led Him to die on the cross to pay for the sins of mankind.

Dear Lord, teach us as parents to be the model you would have us be for our children. Amen.
*NIV

Thirty Seven

The Little Nurse

"Time to have your bottle," I heard from the downstairs playroom. "Then it will be time to go to sleep." Joyous voices from the play- hospital assured me that my daughter and her friends found contentment in running a pretend Pediatric Ward in their make-believe hospital. Each doll had their name pinned to their doll beds, complete with age, and the local Doctor's name. Our daughter frequently reminded us, "I am going to be a nurse someday, you know." This dream never faded. Years passed. The day came when we attended her graduation. The play room downstairs vanished. The make believe patients disappeared. The new Registered Nurse boasted an authentic nurses cap of her own.

We, as parents, want to see our children succeed and achieve their dreams. We want them to have a future of success and hope. Proverbs 22:6* states, "Train up a child in the way he should go and when he is old he will not depart from it." I trust it was not we who influenced our daughter to choose a nursing career. Our role as parents leaves a strong impression; perhaps more than we realize. We want our children to follow the path they choose; not the path that we as parents may wish them to follow. That path may be driven by our own goals that never materialized.

"How great is the love the Father has lavished on us, that we should be called the children of God." states 1 John 3:1* We are beloved children in God's eyes. He is our protector just as we wish Him to protect our children. All of us, with childlike faith, need His guidance, discipline, and love. Do our children see that we consistently follow God's leading in our life? It is vital that we set an example of a God fearing parents for our children. May we, as our daughter did, ask God to direct in our decisions.

Dear Lord, may we live expectantly for your guidance throughout our lives. Amen.

*NIV

Thirty Eight

Trials and Tranquility

"*D*addy, can you bend?", asked our almost-two-year old daughter. Her father had just returned from a hundred-day stay in the hospital due to a heart attack. We had lived in a new parish for six weeks. The excitement of living in a different province, a new home to us, a new school, and new friends led us to think we were on a holiday. The love shown the new Pastor and his family by the congregation was overwhelming. But my husband awakened me early on a Monday morning. He was experiencing a heart attack. A policeman stopped our speeding car driven by a neighbour. We then had police escort the remaining way to the hospital. Days ahead were heavy as my husband hovered between life and death. Willing new friends cared for our children. I spent long days at his bedside, praying constantly for his recovery.

We were elated when my husband returned home. Our youngest promptly took her father's wallet out of my purse and handed it to her father. It fell to the floor. She had no idea that a father who just lived in a bed, could actually bend to pick up a wallet. My husband was granted seven more years to be with his family, but the majority of those days were spent living in a bed. The bedroom became the pastor's office. Confirmation classes, members seeking counsel, and church matters kept the Pastor occupied on "good" days. Coffee was frequently served in the bedroom. The time came when I could drive my husband a few yards to the Sunday church service where he gave a five minute message. I immediately had to drive him home to rest. The support and love of church members shown their Pastor and family never failed.

I felt powerless and anxious, fearing the present as well as the future. But I Peter 5:7* comforted me, "Cast all your anxiety on Him because He cares for you."

Lord, thank you for peace despite trials and tribulation. Amen.
*NIV

Christmas Day at the Hospital

"What is a little girl like your doing in a taxi cab on Christmas morning?" asked the caring taxi driver. "You should be home opening your presents."

Our youngest daughter was six years old. She shyly moved closer to her big brother sitting beside her and replied, "My Daddy is very sick in the hospital. The doctor will let us visit him because it is Christmas." I noticed the driver wipe a tear from his cheek as he tenderly looked down at the wee girl beside him. We had spent Christmas Eve night in a strange hotel in an unfamiliar city.

Christmas carols greeted us as we walked down the sterile hallways. Christmas trees were glowing in various locations. "There is a festive atmosphere here," I remember thinking. "How fortunate for those who can be happy this day. We cannot." The children, due to their father's serious illness, could only spend brief moments at his bedside. Caring staff seemed to sense a father's despair at his inability to show his four dear children how much he loved them.

I remember asking myself, "Why does my dear husband have to be so ill?" I realized the reality of life is that we will all experience suffering and separation at one time or the other in our lives. I am at a loss to know how I could ever cope through chaotic times with out God in my life. I would not know what to do or where to turn. Only God can give us hope and comfort. God gave us courage and strength that day at the General Hospital. He reminds us each Christmas of His gift of the Christ Child who came that we might have eternal life in Him.

Luke 2:10* tells us, "But the angel said to them, 'Do not be afraid. I bring you good news of great joy that will be for all people.'"

Lord, thank you for Your gift of the Christ Child. Amen.
*NIV

Forty

Easter Memories

"*D*addy can't die yet," cried our nine-year-old daughter. "I didn't say goodbye to him!" It was on a Maundy Thursday, the eve before Jesus's death on the cross, that God called a loving husband and father from his life here on earth. I remember my broken heart reminded me of the dark events that led to Good Friday. The death of a loved one taught me emphatically that life is brief, and fragile.

My mind drifted back to younger years when dreams excited me. My dreams included a God fearing prince to be at my side. "But dear Lord," I prayed, "I do not wish to marry a preacher." I had vivid memories of sad pastors' farewells in our Church. It wasn't easy to say goodbye to beloved pastors' families. However, God did bless my life with the gift of love of a young pastor. My desires were no longer in conflict with God's will for my life. God brought a passing acquaintanceship into a lasting relationship. This gift of finding a deep understanding of our hearts; the commitment to become partners in love, became ours.

My reverie finally brought me back to reality. Easter is a time for us to reflect on the gift of life. We can rejoice in the resurrection. It proclaims to us the finality of death is gone. It tells us that in Christ we shall all rise from the grave and live forever with Him. When Christ returns all believers who are dead and alive will be reunited.

"Brothers, we do not want you to be ignorant about those who fall asleep, or grieve like the rest of men, who have no hope. We believe that Jesus died and rose again, and so we believe that God will bring with Jesus those who have fallen asleep in him." 1 Thessalonians 4:13*.

Dear Lord, thank you for dying on the cross, opening the doors to new life to all who accept You as their personal Saviour. Amen. *NIV

Forty One

Diligence

How do you tell a sixteen-year-old son that his Dad just passed away? It was ten 10'clock in the evening. Our son soon disappeared. I found him later sitting on a swing in the neighbouring playground. How does a mother convince a thirteen-year-old son that biking on dirt roads, attempting to make money on selling Regal cards to neighbours, on a sultry, hot day is hard work? How does a mother convince their son that she could take time from her full time work to drive him to the city to bring home his new bike? My son caught a ride to the city, and biked the fifty-five miles home, with only a water jug at his side. How does a mother assure their son that she can help pay for his University education? He managed, with short-term jobs, to pay for it himself. That was our only son. We were blessed to have him in our midst for seventeen more years before he joined his Dad in heaven.

"Sons are a heritage from the Lord, children a reward from him. Like arrows in the hands of a warrior, are sons born in one's youth." Psalm 127:3-4* God gave our son and his sisters life. God gave our son and his sisters as a reward to us.

I have wished, time and again, that I could have lived past years differently when our children were young. Business can be our enemy. We plan our own schedules with our own twenty four hours. We do what we feel is most important to us. Saturdays, when you are at work all week, was a time to catch up on housework, and laundry. I remember on several occasions turning down my son's request, when he was home from university, to go for a cup of coffee on a Saturday. I have difficulty coping with "I should have." I leave that with God!

Dear Lord, forgive us for the times we fail to show loved ones how much we love them. Amen.
*NIV

Forty Two

Believing is So Simple

"I felt so guilty, "stated my daughter, "I hadn't asked God to make Daddy better the last time he went to the hospital." Tears trickled down her cheeks as she continued, "I always prayed that Daddy would soon feel well each time he went to the hospital before. I thought it was my fault Daddy died."

I listened, with a heavy heart some time later, to my daughter's memories of the evening her father passed away. "I felt I wasn't good enough. Why should God listen to me?" She went on to express her teenage feelings of not belonging to her church family. Christianity to her felt so complicated and conditional. Being a creative thinker growing up in a very open minded generation, her perception of Christianity was conflicting and confusing. "It was easier to not get involved than to pretend to be involved. I felt the expectation of church life was demanding and old fashioned."

It was when my daughter realized that becoming a child of God was simply a choice on her part, her view of Christianity changed. I believe she was led by the Holy Spirit to admit passed sins, her complete trust and belief in Jesus who died on the cross for her sins, and her willingness to confess to others that she trusted God henceforth to be in charge of her life.

Perhaps you, too, may identify with my daughter's reactions to Christianity? Do you have feelings of inadequacy when you face the wish to become a child of God? I trust the following Bible passages will reveal to you the simplicity of becoming a child of God.

Mark 1:15b* "Repent and believe."

Romans10:9* "That if you confess with your mouth, ' Jesus is Lord,' and believe in your heart that God raised him from the dead, you will be saved."

Dear Lord, You love us unconditionally. Help us to realize that we are good enough to come to you just as we are. Amen.
*NIV

Forty Three

I'll Meet You in the Morning

"Was it actually that many years ago," I asked myself, "Since I had to say an earthly good bye to my husband?" I have memories of clearing his bureau drawers. I remember tears flowing intermittently as I boxed white shirts. I was reminded of my exasperation, as a preacher's wife, in attempting to master the skill of ironing a shirt to perfection. I, sitting in the back church pew with our children, was my worst critic when it came to judging the appearance of the pastor's shirt collar. I remember removing coloured shirts that brought back memories; the red plaid had reminded me of camping family days, a red shirt used for hunting, and a grease stained shirt was used for car maintenance jobs. The black preacher's socks had a drawer of their own. But what I remember most vividly was a parcel addressed to me in the bottom drawer. Tucked under a new zippered writing case was a square package wrapped carefully in gift paper. I remember tenderly unwrapping the gift. A long-playing record, featuring my husband's favourite male quartet, was sacredly held in my hands. I read the title of the record across the jacket, "I'll Meet You in the Morning."

Living through the grief process is not easy. Grief is unavoidable. It is an unpredictable part of life. There is nothing that prepares us for the death of a loved one. Scripture has plenty of meaningful verses that bring comfort to anyone going through grief. God has left them with us to bring peace and hope when we are crushed under the weight of sorrow. Psalm 147:3* tells us, "He heals the brokenhearted and binds up their wounds." John 16:22* also tells us, "So with you: Now is your time of grief, but I will see you again and you will rejoice, and no one will take away your joy." Only God understands and knows our grief.

Dear Lord, thank you for walking with me through my grief journey. Amen.

*NIV

Forty Four

Storms in Life

"This is strange, my legs still feel numb, Mom," exclaimed my fourteen old daughter. "They have felt numb for the past month." The Doctor questioned if her jeans might be too tight. We realized later that our Doctor was kind to not label her disease until he was convinced it be accurate. The diagnosis of Multiple Sclerosis was not confirmed until she was in Nurse's training. Multiple Sclerosis is one of the most common neurological diseases involving the central nervous system. Periodic sessions of blindness, loss of mobility, and just not feeling well were difficult to endure for a young girl who enjoyed an active life. Steroids were effective but with steroids come side effects.

As a mother and a widow, I felt alone and forlorn. My dreams for a daughter with so much potential crumbled before me. It was then I realized that only Christ could replace my desperation with peace. I prayed for acceptance of my daughter's diagnosis. My daughter, despite the malady that affected her, maintained her zeal for life that motivated her to live each day with a cheerful smile. She accepted her diagnosis more quickly than her mother.

God has not promised us a life free from stress and worry, but He has promised to always be with us. He asks us to bring our concerns to Him, and then believe that He will carry us through the storms of life that we may face on our life's journey. Perhaps you have experienced trials that have caused you to be disheartened and sorrowful? Our joy and thankfulness to God should not fluctuate with our circumstances. Now I ask God, "How can I witness to others when they go through difficult times in their lives?

We read in Psalm 55:22,* "Cast your cares on the Lord and he will sustain you; he will never let the righteous fail."

Dear Lord, we pray for strength to rejoice in all circumstances so your name will be glorified. Amen.
*NIV

Forty Five

The Art of Aging

"Are you saying I was the one chosen to be the Football Queen?", asked the 93 year old resident of our Nursing Home, "I thought some one old would have been selected." Elderly people are delightful. It was a privilege for me to work with the aged. People enter a Nursing Home, when they are unable to cope in their own homes, to live and not to die. Their most excellent quality of life should be maintained until the day they leave this earth.

Aging is a beautiful gift from God. The elderly have knowledge and wisdom to share with the younger generations. Their experiences can be a secret treasury of guidance as young people leave the comfort of their parental home, and venture out into the world. The aged among us are a blessing so we need to include their council to guide us. Our parents, grandparents, and our great grandparents have left us a legacy of upholding God's message of His son giving His life to die for our sin from generation to generation. We are blessed to be included in this Christian heritage.

How comfortable are we with our own aging? Why do many advertisements continually advocate products to delay evidence of aging? Why are we hesitant to tell others our age? We all, in time, will age. God has promised to care for us every year of our life. We, too, are to show compassion and love to the elderly in our care. Isaiah 46:4* says, "Even to your old age and grey hairs I am he, I am he who will sustain you. I have made you and I will carry you; I will sustain you and I will rescue you. May we obey Ephesians 6: 2-3*, "Honour your Father and Mother-which is the first commandment with a promise that it may go well with you and that you may enjoy long life on earth."

Dear Lord, help us to respect, and lovingly care for the elderly among us. Amen.
*NIV

Forty Six

I Trust You, God!

"Mom, I had the scare of my life," my son told me, "It was raining so we were not working. I was sitting under a tree reading when the Cook yelled at me to climb up the tree as a bear was heading toward me." He went on to tell me that the Cook had to shoot the bear. My son was planting trees in the northern part of the province during the summer University break. My hardworking son was proud of the fact he had planted 1200 trees one day. I was concerned when he told me his sleeping bag fell out of the helicopter on the way to the camp. But his narrow escape from the advances of a dangerous bear startled me. I was filled with thankfulness to an almighty God who saved my son from harm.

We are God's children. We are blessed to know that God does protect us. We, as parents, protect our children as much as we are capable to do so. We try to prevent them from falling when they are learning to walk. We keep articles, like scissors, out of their reach. Even so, our Heavenly Father cares for us just as we care for our children. We can be sure God protects us from danger often without our knowledge. Perhaps our prayer requests have not been granted to us, but we realized later that it was for our own good.

Rejections can be difficult to accept, but later we discover they were a blessing. God can see what we cannot see. Proverbs 19:21* tells us, "Many are the plans in a man's heart, but it is the Lord's purpose that prevails." Jesus never ceases to care and protect us. Have you not arrived home and then learned of an accident on the road you just travelled on less than an hour go? God does care!

Dear Lord, thank you for the comfort of knowing your promise to be with us at all times. Amen.
*NIV

Forty Seven

Peace

A late night phone call abruptly awakened me, "Mom, Wes passed away." The hesitant voice of my daughter-in-law continued, "He had a heart attack while playing hockey. The doctors worked on him for two hours but they couldn't save his life."

My reaction to the death of our only son was total unbelief. "Wes is only thirty three years old," I cried in anguish, "We need him, especially his two little children." Mourning the loss of a child has to be one of life's loneliest and most painful experiences. The deep devastating sorrow cut to the core of my being. Wes's father had passed away in a like manner when Wes was fifteen years old.

Only heavy grey clouds floated above me for the ensuing days. "Dear God," I prayed, "Where are you?" I yearned for the assurance of His presence. Work was therapy for me so I attacked our storeroom. Then to my surprise, tucked behind jars of pickles and jam, was a wall hanging a young lad had brought home for his mother. The message simply stated, "Peace Be With You." I clasped the splintered board to my bosom. God's loving arms surrounded me with a sense of powerful peace. His presence comforted me.

God has not promised that we will be exempt from sorrow and death in this life. We are all going to eventually die. But He has promised to be with us, grant us courage, comfort and peace. Only God can bring solace and rest. Life goes on. Each day is a gift from God. God has promised to give us peace in the midst of trials that we have to face in this life.

"Peace I leave with you; peace I give to you. I do not give to you as the world gives, do not let your hearts be troubled, and do not let them be afraid." John 14:27*.

Dear Lord, thank you for comforting us with peace when we meet sorrow and pain on our journey through life. Amen.
*NIV

Forty Eight

Grief

"Dear Lord," I prayed, "I feel as though I have reached the bottom of despair." I was on my way home from my son's funeral. What right did the people on the streets, as I drove by, have permission to be jovial? Why was a musician allowed to play a merry tune outside of the Music Store? My world was shattered. Didn't they understand? My son's death had struck me like a tidal wave. I was alone. My son's father had also passed away from a heart attack. The road loomed ahead of me out into the impending darkness. Farm lights began to glimmer mockingly. Then, to my astonishment, an illuminated cross on a village church came into my view. "God, you are with me. You know my sorrow." The cross, where Jesus suffered and died for my sins, spoke to me. God was near!

I knew that I, in time, would have to accept my son's death. Denial was now no choice. It was difficult to accept reality. I began to realize that I had been so blessed to have had my son in my life for thirty three years. I became more aware of my daughters who were hurting. Time is a healer but being told this fact is of no comfort when when grief first strikes. As time goes by, relatives' and friends' lives go back to normal but mine did not. Working through grief is hard, and takes time, but is necessary. Only God can deliver us from grief and despair.

Perhaps you may identify with my reactions if you have also had to cope with death in your family. There is a bond of understanding when you meet someone who has also experienced the loss of a child.

"The Lord is closer to the brokenhearted and he saves those who are crushed in spirit." Psalm 34:18*.

Dear Lord, thank you, as the Psalmist says, for being with me as I walked through the valley of death. Amen.
*NIV

Forty Nine

Two Little Shoes

Withered and worn thin on busy happy feet; two little shoes shriveled and parched with age appear lifeless; brittle to my touch.

Memories of years gone by pierce my wounded heart; a sad reminder of happily running feet joyously active feet bereft of care but now silenced in our home.

Appreciative am I, God, for your gift of a son lent to me momentarily to love and cherish. Did caring so deeply increase my anguish?

Miraculously God comforts me; reveals heaven is now closer to me.

Blessed am I to know my son awaits me in glory to live forever more. So thank you, God, for two little shoes – momentous of your great gift to me.

Saying an earthly good bye to a child brings grief beyond measure. The wounded heart of a parent understands the depth of sorrow such sadness can bring. Psalm 121:1-3, 5-8* confirms God's love and presence as we travel this rocky road. "I lift up my eyes to the hills – where does my help come from? My help comes from the Lord, the Maker of heaven and earth. He will not let your foot slip – he who watches over you will not slumber. The Lord watches over you – the Lord is your shade at your right hand; the sun will not harm you by day, nor the moon by night. The Lord will keep you from all harm- he will watch over your life; the Lord will watch over your coming and going both now and forever more."

Grief can be never ending, especially for a parent. How do people cope who have no faith in God? It is our Lord that comforts us, gives us courage and peace, hastening our healing process. Scripture helps us understand that illness and death are a part of life. We will meet our own demise some day. God helps us cope with our loss, gives us strength and hope to go on.

Lord, thank you for bestowing your grace and mercy on us. Amen.
*NIV

Fifty

God's Message

Travelling in Norway, shortly after the death of our son, did not hasten my recovery through my grief process. I brought my grief with me. I was especially moved by our trip through the mountains. I penned my thoughts on my note pad as our bus wove in zigzag fashion through the narrow trails.

My Supplication

"The language of God's lofty mountains
speaks of majesty, beauty and might.
They stand adorned with snow-capped crowns
set with jewels, glistening and bright.

Proud peaks peer through the hovering clouds
approaching cosmic heavens above.
With arms outstretched to God's galaxy, yet
a haven for the wren and the dove.

Oh, that I, Lord, could climb to such heights,
soar above in the vast sea of blue.
Fly way up high with grief-free wings? And
have happiness and joy anew?

My tears flow as springs of the mountain. Will
they, too, Lord, refresh and refine?
May my healing then come more swiftly after
the loss of the lad that was mine?

But, dear Lord, is this then your message,
conveyed down to me from heights above,
'Without the dark walk in the valley, you'd
not know the summit of my love?'"

We read in Psalm 46:1*, "God is our refuge and strength, an
ever present help in trouble." Only God can give us strength and
peace.

Lord, thank you for giving us strength to go on when we face
grief. Amen.
*NIV

Fifty One

A Miracle

"My right arm feels numb, Mom," stated my eldest daughter in alarm one evening. "I do not feel well, I am going to bed." In less than an hour, her lips were blue and her skin felt cold and clammy. Nausea and dizziness soon attacked her. My daughter, in faltering speech, uttered, "My head aches. I can't even lift my head."

Doctors performed test after test at our local hospital. Blood pressure increased, and body temperature soared. We made the hour trip to the University Hospital in the early hours. My daughter seemingly slept beside me as I drove into the night. She didn't respond when I attempted to speak with her. I spent the day with my daughter, in a semiconscious state, in a cubicle of a busy Emergency Room. "Dear God," I repeatedly prayed, "Please heal my dear daughter." Strict isolation due to a possible diagnoses of Meningitis was put into practice. Long and lonely hours as I sat by her bedside gave me the time to pray. A kind Security Guard walked me to an adjacent residence in the late hours each evening.

But God was working a miracle of healing through the skilful knowledge of expert Doctors. "We have hope for your daughter's recovery," stated a Doctor one morning. "We now know your daughter has Encephalitis. We have a drug that is specific for this illness. We will give it intravenously for a ten-day period." Each day saw improvement as the miracle drug was administered. Her ready smile, as she responded to our voices, brought a prayer of thanksgiving and praise to a loving God for His healing. God performs miracles today just as He did in Bible times. We are blessed.

We read in Matthew 42:23*., "Jesus went throughout Galilee, teaching in their synagogues, preaching the good news of the kingdom, and healing every disease and sickness among the people."

Dear Lord, thank you for asking us to bring all our concerns to you. Amen.
*NIV

Fifty Two

Sundowning

Do you remember, as a child, the first time you had a sleepover? Do you remember, at around supper time, feeling home sick for Mom and Dad? My parents thought their six- year- old could stay with the teacher at the home of an aged lady who lived near a country school. It was my first experience of attending Vacation Bible School. Days went fine, but I have memories of missing home when supper time arrived. The unfamiliar environment increased my homesickness. I was a lonely youngster with a stomach ache.

I was reminded of my experience as a child when working with the aged in a Nursing Home. Several of our residents became very restless and anxious at dusk. The transition from daylight to darkness saw a few residents experience periods of confusion, and loss of memory. Seniors recovering from surgery have been known to experience this Sundowning Syndrome, especially because they are in a new environment. Offering assurance to the resident that they are safe, and will not be left alone usually gives the comfort and support they require. Distracting the elder by going for a walk, and exploring the grounds with their care giver can be reassuring therapy.

We read in Isaiah 41:10*,"Do not fear for I am with you, do not be dismayed for I am your God. I will strengthen you and I will help you; I will uphold you with my righteous right hand." How blessed we are to know God has promised to be with us anytime we feel lonely and restless, regardless of what the circumstances may be. Many scripture passages remind us of God's presence to guide and protect us be we a small child, a teenager or an adult that meets fearful and lonely situations. Our relationship with Jesus brings rest and peace. Godly care givers Jesus places in our lives witness to us of His love. Use me, Lord, to comfort another.

Dear Lord, thank you for your promise to be with us throughout our lives. Amen.
*NIV

Fifty Three

Faithfulness

No one guessed that our Mother attended an Evening Mid Week service at her church with a wee dog tucked under her sweater. Mother was dog sitting. My Aunt's chocolate dog, named Coccoa, was having a sleepover while her mistress was away. Our faithful Mother never wanted to miss a church service. "I knew it wasn't a dogs place to be in church," she later confessed, "but I told Cocoa that he couldn't make a sound, and he didn't." Apparently no one caught on to the four legged attendee tucked warmly inside a dark sweater. And Mother never missed church.

Proverbs 3:3-4* tells us,"Let love and faithfulness never leave you; bind them around your neck, write them on the tablet of your heart. Then you will win favour and a good name in the sight of God and man." This was our Mother. Her love and faithfulness was evident by her actions at all times. Her attitude was an attitude of giving of herself to be faithful in God's service. It was Mother who convinced Dad to drive her to an aged neighbour who wasn't the best housekeeper. It was Mother who heard of a couple, new to the community, who had both been ill. Mother worked in the house while Dad helped the husband with his chores. Faithfulness and love are God given characteristics.

God rewards us with many blessings. We need to spend time in His Word and in prayer. Even if we are going through deep valleys and God seems far away, we are to remember that He never leaves us. It is we that have drifted away. I have precious memories in my mind of seeing my Mother bent over her Bible at her dining room table, hands folded and eyes closed, in prayer to her Lord. She continued to spend this time with her Lord despite the advancement of Dementia. But I am sure God understood her!

Dear Lord, may we never become weary in doing good in your service. Amen.
*NIV

Fifty Four

Royalty

$\mathcal{N}$ames are our identity. Is it not our name the greatest connection to our individuality? Is it also the very heart of our own existence? Our name is very important to us. Just miss spell some one's name or pronounce it incorrectly. You will soon be corrected. The name "Beatrice" meant "Mother" to our family. We were blessed to know that our Mother brought each of her children's names to the throne of God daily.

My Mother was delighted, back in 1988, to read in the Regina Leader Post of the birth of a daughter born to the Duke and Duchess of York. They named her, Princess Beatrice Elizabeth Mary. The article went on to say the last Princess Beatrice among British royals was the youngest of Queen of Victoria's nine children. Mother, then in her eighties, told us she had never known a baby to be named Beatrice. She then proceeded to lovingly put together a baby quilt, edged with pink braid, for this royal child. Each stitch into this delicate quilt, made of material covered with dainty roses, was stitched with love. "I am praying for little Beatrice" was written on the card that was tucked inside the gift. Mother was delighted to receive a letter from the Lady in Waiting stating,

"The Duchess of York has asked me to write and thank you very much for the wonderful present you sent on the arrival of her baby, Princess Beatrice of York. Her Royal Highness was extremely touched by your kindness and generosity and I am to convey her sincere thanks." God gave Mother more years to bring her children by name to the throne of grace. How rich we were to be remembered by name with royalty in prayer each day.

Isaiah 43:1b* states, "Fear not, for I have redeemed you; you are mine. I have summoned you by name; you are mine." We are important to God. We are blessed.

Dear Lord, thank you for knowing us individually, even knowing us by name! Amen.
*NIV

Our Saint

"Mom, my friend and her Mom are coming to visit," exclaimed our eldest daughter, "She just phoned to tell me they are coming out here for sure." We had arranged a bus trip to a neighbouring town days earlier with the anticipation that we could go on this trip together. However, our daughter had applied to start a new job at a local business. Word came that orientation was to be on the same day as the bus trip. My heart attacks me each time I think of that day, which occurred years ago, that I should have influenced my dear daughter not to keep this orientation appointment. She loyally stayed home, walked uptown to the business, knowing she was missing a wonderful opportunity to be with her friend. I was stabbed with another feeling of guilt when the position she hoped to have didn't work out. This daughter, time and again, forgives with a magnitude of love that overwhelms me. I have asked her, time and again, to forgive me if I have been impatient. "That's alright, Mom," she would say with a smile, "I am used to it."

Jesus tells us that we are to be child-like, with sincere and humble hearts in Matthew 18:3-4:*, "And he said, 'I tell you the truth, unless you change and become like little children, you will never enter the kingdom of heaven. Therefore, whoever humbles himself like this child is the greatest in the kingdom of heaven.'" We realize that we do influence the people entrusted to our care. Are we constantly loving to others? Are there times when we should have given a hug instead of a scolding? Are we ready to forgive, a conscious and deliberate decision to release feelings of resentment, toward a person? We may have difficulty forgiving ourselves when feelings of guilt attacks us. God is waiting to forgive and guide us as we bring all our concerns to Him.

Dear Lord, may we love others based on Your sacrificial love for us. Amen.
*NIV

Fifty Six

Recovering the Lost

"I lost it!" I exclaimed to my elderly Mother. "I lost my favourite earring." I had just returned from a Norwegian course I was taking at the University. I was wearing earrings purchased in Hawaii while vacationing with my daughters. The Flea-marked price was unbelievable. Was it selfish of me to pray that I might find the lost earring? I traced my tracks back to search. I thought of the verse in Genesis 18:14a*, "Is anything too hard for the Lord?" A search of the classroom finally brought a crushed earring to sight. I thanked God for helping me find my treasure as I drove home.

I was happy to tell my Mother that the lost was found. Her response came quickly,"I am glad as I surely wasn't going to bother God with a mere earring." But I did bother God with such a request. I was grateful to God who permitted me to bring anything and everything to Him in prayer. I was thankful even if I found out later that it cost more to repair the one earring than I had initially paid for the two of them in Hawaii. But I know He hears my requests, and answers my prayers according to His will. I do not always realize why my requests are not always granted but I know God knows best.

There is a verse in 1 Chronicles 16:34* that says, "Give thanks to the Lord, for he is good; his love endures forever." Do you realize how much we have to be thankful for? We can bring any need or concern to God, be it the loss of keepsake, a treasure with emotional ties or a displaced credit card. God hears all our requests. God understands any turmoil we may experience. He is waiting to be of service if we but trust Him, and leave all our concerns at His feet. We are blessed!

Dear Lord, thank you for hearing and answering our prayers each time we call on you. Amen.
*NIV

Fifty Seven

Panic and Peace

My body trembled, and my hands felt cold and clammy. I was abruptly awakened in the midst of a frightening dream, a dream of fear and danger for my daughter who was travelling in Greece. "Dear God," I prayed, "Protect her where ever she might be." I frantically prayed for her safety. Sleep eluded me at first. But I found, as I prayed, a feeling of peace slowly overwhelmed me.

My hand shook as I lifted the receiver when a phone call came from Greece later in the day. My daughter had boarded a crowded bus. The driver had turned abruptly on the side of steep hill. "Mom, everyone gasped in shock as the right wheels lifted from the road. All I could see was the dark water lashing against the rocks below." A thankful voice continued, "Only a miracle enabled the bus driver to get those wheels back on the road." I shed a tear when the faint voice of my daughter continued, "You must have been praying for me, Mom." My heart filled with praise and thanksgiving to my heavenly Father. I was overcome with awe and yet gratitude to realize that God led me to pray for my daughter's safety in the night.

God asks us to cast all our cares and concerns on Him. We fail God when we insist on shouldering our burdens and fears instead of giving them to the Lord. He promises joy, peace and rest when we place ourselves in God's hands. God tells us not to worry but to pray. God alone can give us peace.

Philippians 4:6-7* tells us, "Do not be anxious about anything, but in everything, by prayer and petition, with thanksgiving, present your request to God. And the peace of God, which transcends all understanding, will guard your hearts and your minds in Christ Jesus."

Dear Lord, we praise You for answered prayer. We are confident that nothing can separate us from your love, protection and guidance. Amen.
*NIV

Fifty Eight

God's Gifts

I heard our eldest daughter singing "Happy Birthday" to someone one morning. I asked her who she was singing to at that hour. Her quick response was, "To Price William, the Duke of Cambridge." She went on to tell me that a documentary on TV had informed her of royalty birthdays. She doesn't require a birthday book. She hears a birthday once and the date remains with her. Relatives tell us that a great aunt had the same gift. We, as a family, contact her any time we require a birth date.

Birth dates are important to us. We, as individuals, are possessive of our claim to the date we entered this world. My Ophthalmologist's secretary confirms my identity each time I visit by requesting to know my birth date. Birthdays are exciting to a child, to a youth who is waiting for teenage years to arrive, and to a young adult who is waiting to make a difference in the world. God gave our daughter the gift of remembering each birth date she hears. I frequently receive the phone call, "Mother, did you remember to send a card to...? Her birthday is next Friday."

A verse in Romans 12:6a* states, "We have different gifts, according to the grace given us." James 1:17a* says, "Every good and perfect gift is from above." God, in His grace, gave us loving gifts when He gave our eldest daughter, her brother and sisters to my husband and me. He gave us a daughter who keeps us informed of what is important to individuals – their birth date.

My childhood memories include our keen joy and anticipation waiting for the Christmas season. The Eaton's Christmas catalogue was dishevelled by the time Christmas arrived. But we celebrate God's greatest gift to us when we celebrate Jesus' birth date. God brought His only Son into the world to die on the cross to pay for your sin and mine.

Lord, thank you for joyous birthday celebrations including Your Son's birth date at Christmas. Amen.
*NIV

Fifty Nine

Moses and Early Mornings

"I am thankful," I thought to myself, "that Moses was not my father." I do not appreciate early morning activities. Evening hours are my most productive time. But Moses, and numerous Biblical men of God, worshipped their Lord early in the morning. The law of Moses, as God directed him, required the Israelis to faithfully make atonement for their sins. God, in the Old Testament, accepted the death of an animal as s substitute for a sinner seeking God's forgiveness. The blood that was shed by an animal was proof that a life had been given for another. Moses, no doubt with his household, made preparations for these rituals in the morning.

The Old Testament relates many more early morning rituals that took place that fulfilled God's commands. We can well imagine the anticipation of faithful followers of God as they waited for the promised coming of the Messiah. Jesus came. Scripture gives us accounts of Jesus, too, rising in the early morning hours to spend time with His Father. Mark 1:35* tells us, "Very early in the morning, while it was still dark, Jesus got up, left the house and went off to a solitary place, where He prayed." Jesus, who knew no sin, found it necessary to be alone with His Father. This fact, reminds me to look to my need to spend time in prayer. Do I think a few hours of sleep are more valuable to me than spending time conversing with the Lord? Old habits can be altered. Moses, in the early morning, fulfilled God's commands in his leadership duties. Help me, O God, to give you my time in the morning.

Scripture tells us, "Moses went and told the people all the Lord's words and laws - 'Everything the Lord has said we will do'. He got up early the next morning and built an alter at the foot of the mountain." Exodus 24:3a, 4b*

Lord, I give my mornings and my days in service for you. Amen.
*NIV

Sixty

We Are Not to Worry

A pair of Finches often claim a perch on the branches of an aspen tree outside my window. Is it my imagination that leads me to believe that the same pair of birds welcome me each time they peer into my living room? Their seemingly content and quiet demeanor gives me a sense of peace and calmness. They, in their swift movements, find the nourishment that God provides for them in His creation. God supplies all their needs.

God admonishes us not to worry and fret concerning our needs. Worry denies God's wisdom and willingness to meet our concerns. Worry brings discouragement and depression. Worry also shows a lack of faith in God. Worry can cause us unhappiness and even effect our health. Our Lord asks us to cast every care and concern at His feet regardless of what the concern may be. We do not have to worry about storing up treasures here on earth. We can easily become too possessed to attain earthly wealth, and forsake spiritual treasures in heaven. God promises to being peace in our lives if we put our complete trust in Him for every need we many have.

My two Finches do not have to worry concerning what they may require in order to live each day. But they have to satisfy their hunger, build nests, wait patiently for their eggs to hatch, and then raise their family. We, also, are responsible to work in order to provide for ourselves and others God has placed in our care. Jesus reminds us that we are more valuable than my Finches. He will supply our every need if we but ask Him and believe that He will do so.

Let us remember Jesus's Words, "Look at the birds of the air: they do not sow or reap or store away in barns, and yet your heavenly Father feeds them. Are you not much more valuable than they?" Matthew 6:26*.

Lord, thank you for your promises to meet our every need. Amen.
*NIV

Sixty One

Crown of Thorns and Easter Blessings

$\mathcal{I}$was awe struck. The crown of thorns plant before me, grown in the shape of a crown, boasted brightly coloured flowers that were exquisite and delicate. The sharp thorns that grow on fleshy brown stems are wicked. According to a legend, a Crown of Thorns plant was given its name after it was associated with the crown of thorns placed on Jesus's head at the time of His crucifixion. The remarkable feature of this plant is that it blooms unceasingly.

Easter memories remind me that Jesus paid the supreme sacrifice for my sins, wearing the Crown of Thorns, with His precious blood shed on the cross. Easter memories of my youth included attending early morning Easter service followed by a scrumptious breakfast. These events in our church were unceasing through out the year just like the consistent blooms of the Crown of Thorns plant.

I am also reminded of the many blessings that have been mine throughout the years. There are times when I have wept when sorrow has given me more pain than I thought I could bare; times when the dark hours of night have eluded sleep from me. I have asked, "God, where are you?" only to eventually realize that my heavenly Father has never forsaken me. I have learned that Christ's love and presence as well as His forgiveness are unceasing just as the Crown of Thorns plant that goes on blooming consistently.

We, too, can bloom by His grace where ever we may be. Perhaps the parents down the street, who lost their only daughter, or the Music Director of the church choir recently diagnosed with cancer require our love and prayer involvement. We, too, can bloom faithfully by His grace as do the blossoms of the Crown of Thorns plant.

"The soldiers twisted together a crown of thorns and put it on his head." John 19:2a*.

Dear Lord, thank you for wearing a Crown of Thorns, and paying the supreme sacrifice for our sins. Amen.
*NIV

Sixty Two

The Holy Land

$\mathcal{A}$we and wonder over come me as I recall, on a visit to Israel, sailing on the sea of Galilee. I have a picture in my mind of blue waves, white floating clouds, and gently sloping hills ascending from the shore. This is the land where Jesus walked. The hills and the firmament that bordered the Sea of Galilee witnessed Jesus performing miracle after miracle. But as I sat in the smooth sailing boat, I remember gazing into the depths of the Sea of Galilee. I was reminded of Mark's account of a turbulent storm that overtook the water when Jesus was asleep on the boat. I have been told that unexpected storms frequented this area. The disciples must have witnessed many such squalls while fishing. However, they were terrified as they were being tossed about, vulnerable to nature's fury. So why were they so terrified when Jesus was with them on the boat?

I was convicted of my own lack of faith when troubles assail me. We all meet trials and difficulties in life. Do we, like the disciples who awakened Jesus, fail to put all our trust in God, not realizing His power to take care of every situation in our lives? God is in control. He is waiting to hear from us when we face trials.

"That day when evening came, he said to his disciples, 'Let us go over to the other side.' Leaving the crowd behind, they took him along, just as he was, in the boat. There were also other boats with him. A furious squall came up, and the waves brook over the boat, so that it was nearly swamped. Jesus was in the stern asleep on a cushion. The disciples woke him and said to him, 'Teacher, don't you care if we drown? He got up and rebuked the wind and said to the waves, 'Quiet! Be still!'" Mark 4:35-39*

Lord, thank you for bringing peace despite storms we may face. Amen.
*NIV

I will Not Forsake You

"Look, Mom, I see a cross up there in the hills!" exclaimed my daughter. It was twilight. My girls and I ventured out for a walk near our strange hotel in a strange city on a European tour. It was Sunday. We never heard church bells resounding throughout the city. People seemed as rushed on the Lord's day as is the trend on week days. Lack of reverence for this day of rest was so apparent. But now we all looked up at the hills. The setting sun had left a transcendent glow on a cross looking down at us. My heart filled with gratitude for a God who lets us know that He never leaves nor forsakes us.

God keeps His promises. I realized my limited awareness of the greatness of the Creator in the evening hours of that Sunday in Europe. Was I just looking for the ordinary, comparing Him to my earthly expectations? The sight of the illuminated cross made me realize more fully that God, mighty and powerful as He is, cares for each one of us personally no matter where we may be. God is omnipresent. I was confident God was with me, and would continue to grant my daughters and myself a safe and enjoyable trip.

God is with you and me when we travel the world, and when we are in our homes. Does it not behoove us to witness to others of our loving God who loves us, was crucified on the cross for us, and watches over us each day? We have a message to tell the world.

God is always with us. "The Lord himself goes before you and will be with you; He will never leave you nor forsake you. Do not be afraid; do not be discouraged." Deuteronomy 31:8*.

Dear Lord, send many to witness of your love, your death on the cross, and your resurrection to the nations. Even send me. Amen.
*NIV

Sixty Four

Help Me Listen and Obey

"Thank you, Lord, it is Friday" I silently prayed. I was weary. I was grateful for the opportunity to work in a position that was enjoyable as well as fulfilling. Now I longed for a relaxing weekend. The phone rang as I prepared to leave. It was a call from the Laundry, "Do you remember when you picked up our unusable linens? An eager voice continued, "You brought them to a lady that makes quilts for the homeless." i sighed as the voice continued, "We have more and we would like to clear them out before the weekend. Is it possible for you to pick them up today?"

"Not today," I reasoned to myself, "Monday and a new week will soon be here." I reached for my coat and was about to lock the office door when a feeling of guilt overcame me. I was overcome with an intense necessity to halt, to reconsider my decision to immediately go home.

"You are an answer to my prayer," exclaimed Annie as I carried the bags into her apartment. "I told God today that I would have to quit sewing quilts if I didn't have more material by tonight." I was shocked at the thought of me, unworthy as I am, to be an answer to Annie's prayer requests. "I have been so discouraged. I have several quilts to finish and I have not had material for them for weeks. "But now," she continued excitingly, "God answered my prayer."

Are we prompt to follow His leading? I was not. I was too concerned with my own desires. Do we take time to pray for someone when God reminds us of them as we go about out daily activities?

"Do not withhold good from those who deserve it, when it is in your power to act. Do not say to your neighbour, "Come back later. I'll give it to you tomorrow.'" Proverbs 3:27-28*.

Lord, may we always listen to your prompting. Amen.
*NIV

Sixty Five

Fear and Faith

"*D*ear Lord," I prayed, "Help me to believe they will not find a trace of cancer." My daughter was in the operating room. Her surgeon was removing a growth from her kidney. My heart pounded rapidly, I felt tense, and worried. I was restless as I sat in her hospital room waiting for the nurses to bring her back to her ward. "Why do I think of the worst outcome at a time like this?" I asked myself. I was fearful, and at the same time frustrated with my lack of faith. I was reminded of a Bible verse in Isaiah 41:10*, "So do not fear, for I am with you; do not be dismayed for I am your God. I will strengthen you and help you; I will uphold you with my righteous right hand."

I realized that it is normal for we human beings to feel frightened. But I realized, too, that I had not put my complete trust in the Lord. Didn't I remember God is in control? "Dear Lord, forgive me for my lack of faith," I prayed,"Help me to put my trust in you." I then turned my anxiety over to God. Isaiah 6:3* tells us "You will keep him in perfect peace whose mind is steadfast, because he trusts in you." Waiting for the diagnoses after the surgery was grueling. But trusting God did bring a sense of peace. My family and I rejoiced with thankfulness when the report finally came back to tell us the growth was benign. God answered my prayers. God is good.

There are many verses in Scripture that request us to put our trust in the Lord. Psalm 94:19* tells us "When anxiety was great within me, your consolation brought joy to my soul." Permitting God to take care of our concerns requires us to put our trust in God. God is good!

Dear Lord, thank you for requesting us to ask you for courage and hope in all our fears and concerns. Amen.
*NIV

Papa's Hands

$\mathcal{I}$ remember Papa's hands as a child –
supporting, gentle, soothing hands
that folded my hands in prayer to God,
lifted me when I stumbled and fell –
tenderly conveying a deep love as sturdy,
comforting hands clasped mine.
I remember Papa's hands when a youth –
strong, steady and powerful hands
that cut ice on the pond in winter so thirsty
cows and horses could drink -
placed blocks of ice in the ice house so
nutritious food was on our table.
I remember Papa's hands when an adolescent –
helpful and capable hands
that hitched Buster to the school cutter,
carried warm ashes to start the car,
built a wind charger so we had lights – we
all could even read at night.

I remember Papa's hands as an adult, busy
hands qualified to multitask, and
that worked that I might train as a nurse,
and paid for our marriage,
touched the lives of his grandchildren -
conveying his love to each one.
Now I remember Papa's hands in death. God
blessed my life through Papa's hands,
that were callused and scarred, and now cold, limp and lifeless.
Use my hands, Oh Lord. You used Papa's hands.

Proverbs 23:22a, 24,"Listen to your father, who gave you life. The father of a righteous man has great joy; he who has a wise son delights in him." We are blessed to have Christian fathers who bring order and discipline to their home. Children look for guidance and direction, even if it may be contrary to their wishes. They know that parents do so because they are loved. A father is the provider for his family. Quality time he spends with his child builds a bond that will be remembered. "How great is the love the Father has lavished on us, that we should be called the children of God." 1 John 3:1*. God is our heavenly Father. How blessed are we to be His children. Thank you, Lord!

Dear Heavenly Father, thank you for loving fathers who love their children unconditionally. Amen.
*NIV

Sixty Seven

But God is Good

*D*ear Lord, I prayed that my first delivery would be without problems but You said No.

Now I know her loving and forgiving spirit enriches every life she touches.

Dear Lord, I prayed that my beloved would be made well but You said No.

Now I know You had a purpose in his death. Some time I'll understand.

Dear Lord, I prayed that our daughter's diagnoses wouldn't be Multiple Sclerosis but You said No.

Now I know her smile and forgiveness inspire others with like disabilities.

Dear Lord, I prayed that our baby would be another brother but You said No.

Now I know we needed a caring daughter with numerous capabilities.

Dear Lord, I prayed that our son wouldn't inherit heart disease but You said No.

Now I know his death brought me closer to You - due to your love and pruning.

Dear Lord, I prayed for fewer moments of grief and despair but you said No.

Now I know You are with me every day. Your bestow me with mercy and grace.

Thank you, Lord, You gave me life, loved me and died for me. I have known love, the gift of children, and the gift of friends. Life isn't always fair but You, God, are good. Amen.

We read in Psalm 100:4-5*, "Enter his gates with thanksgiving and his courts with praise; give thanks to him and praise his name. For the Lord is good and his love endures forever; his faithfulness endures through all generations." God knows the pain I have suffered. He knows the tears I have shed. But God did not desert me. In the midst of the storms that I have had to face, God was with me. He has not left me alone during my hardest moments even though I have asked, "Why God?" Now I have asked Him, "What for God?" God is my refuge.

Dear Lord, thank you for your presence with us when we go through the valleys on our life's journey. Amen.
*NIV

Growing Older

"Please put my eye drops in a bag," I asked the Pharmacist, "I am walking and I do not have a purse with me." I was happy with my stamina when it came to this form of exercise.

"You are walking in this cold weather," exclaimed the Pharmacist, "A lady just told me that she froze her ear walking here and she was young." I stepped back. I was reminded of a message I read on a wall hanging, "We start by growing old in other peoples eyes. Then slowly we come to share their judgment." Did I really look that old? I dwelt on the concept of my aging with every step as I made my way home from the Drug Store. I scolded myself as I realized that I had to admit I was getting older.

It is the natural order of life that we should eventually age. Many are denied it when, in their youth, they succumb due to various causes. We read of blessed biblical saints, as Abraham and Moses, who accomplished much for God in their later years. Old age can soften the heart, bring quietness and serenity to a former busy life, and provide opportunities for reaching new goals. God, in His goodness, gives us a gift when He gives us an extended time to live for Him, and to enjoy the people we love. God never ages. He is with us every stage in our life. Let us live dedicating our days in service for Him. There is no limit to God's love for us.

Life can be fruitful as long as we live. I am touched by the ninety year old who fearlessly looks into the future, waiting for His Saviour to take him "home."

"Even to your old age and grey hairs I am he, I am he who will sustain you. I have made you and I will carry you" Isaiah 46:4a*.

Dear Lord, help us to live for you from youth to old age. Amen.
*NIV

Retirement

"So when are you going to retire?" This question on a bright May morning struck me with surprise. Retire? I enjoyed my work. Each day was filled with purpose and good job satisfaction. I felt that my work was the centre of my identity. Social life was enhanced by positive interaction with co- workers. I would loose contact with these people. Retire? I would have to think about that. Did the question imply that it was about time for me to retire? Did people believe that I was not performing at my maximum? Perhaps this suggestion threatened my self esteem. Could it be that retirement rests ultimately on a social judgment that the interests of society are better served by excluding older people from work positions?

Everyone, as long as we have breath, will age in time. My positive soul searching was encouraged by the thought that retirement can be an opportunity. I decided that henceforth I would not think of retiring "from" but what I could be retiring "to." God promised in Psalm92:14-15*. "They will still bear fruit in old age, they will stay fresh and green, proclaiming 'The Lord is upright, he is my Rock, and there is no wickedness in him.'"

Here was my opportunity to be challenged to "grow" in different areas following God's leading.

You may be young with promising dreams ahead of you. Perhaps you are now striving to meet those expectations with God as your guide. Somehow, our interests of our youth continue to be uppermost in our minds when we reach time for retirement. Aging begins at the moment of birth and it ends when life itself has ended. I concluded in my mind that I would look forward to retirement; I will retire and revive. You and I can claim new and happy moments as we have the time to appreciate opportunities that God will provide.

Lord, may we seek your guidance for our life from birth to post retirement days. Amen.
*NIV

Seventy

Joy Unspeakable

"Dear Lord," I had prayed after years of widowhood, "If it is not your will that I will never marry again, remove this longing to have a husband to love." I had recently retired. The children had now left home. God did not remove this sincere yearning of my heart. God did answer my prayer. We met at church; two lonely people who had said an earthly good bye to our spouses. Finding love again rekindled a deep serge of joy. I never thought it possible to find such deep happiness again. Saying an earthly good bye to an endearing soul mate is painful. To find such deep love again was beyond my expectation. Adjustments were few. Supportive family members hastened bonding. Life was good. We were blessed beyond expectation.

"I never thought you had it in you," was the surprised remark by my teen age neighbour. I realized that being an older bride is not the norm as far as the younger generation is concerned. Courtship and marriage, as we know it in our early years, takes on a different tempo when our hair is turning grey. However, God has given us the gift to know the deep satisfaction of having someone to love, and to be a recipient of that love in return at any age.

Mere words cannot adequately describe the extent of happiness that was mine.

Psalm 37:4* tells us, "Delight yourself in the Lord and he will give you the desires of your heart."

We are to put our complete trust in Him believing that He will answer our prayers as we delight in Him according to His will. God knows our need. We may have to wait patiently for answers to our prayers. Our timing is not always the Lord's timing. Just as we who are parents want to give our children what they long for, our heavenly Father delights to give us the desires of our heart.

Lord, thank you for we are of all people most blessed. Amen.
*NIV

Seventy One

Joy Beyond Measure

I had long longed for an RV. I had dreamed of our family owning a "holiday home" on wheels. I admired driving past homes with an RV parked in their driveway. This dream never became a reality for me. Year after year quickly passed. Then, to my happiness, love entered this widow's life. One day an RV was parked in my driveway. My friend welcomed me to go on a day trip to explore an area of the province that was unfamiliar to me. He came with a lunch that we enjoyed in a park in a small village. Our married life included numerous trips that were enjoyed in the comfort of this RV. Each trip was an adventure, and each trip created memories that linger with me. God blessed me with more than an RV in my life. I was blessed with a husband that I could love and cherish.

No matter how old we are or how long we have been waiting, we can live the dreams that have been uppermost in our thoughts for years. We all require hope in our lives. We know definitely what we want. Does God put desires in our hearts that He, in His wisdom, wishes us to have? We read in Psalm 37:5*, "Commit your way to the Lord, trust in him and he will do this." We are to delight our selves in God, put Him first in our lives. 1 John 5:14-15* also states, "This is the confidence we have in approaching God: that if we ask anything according to his will, he hears us. And if we know that he hears us – whatever we ask of him – we know that we have what we asked of him." The more we commit ourselves to the Lord, the more our joy is complete. We free ourselves by turning all our cares and requests to God, fully trusting Him to take care of us.

Dear Lord, thank you for answering our prayers according to your will. Amen.
*NIV

Seventy Two

Receive and Share

"*P*lease buy white eggs when you go shopping," my husband told me shortly after we were married. "I prefer them to brown eggs." My husband had operated a Grocery Store in the northern area of the province. Farmers brought their fresh brown eggs and their older brown eggs to the store in exchange for groceries. These eggs accumulated as egg sales were limited when many of the farmers raised their own chickens. It was necessary periodically for the generous storekeeper to load eggs into his stationwagon, and distribute them to people in the community who welcomed this gift. A bakery in a neighbouring town always had need for eggs. These actions of their storekeeper were appreciated by the community. His caring attitude toward shoppers didn't go unnoticed.

We read in 11 Corinthians 9:11-13*, "You will be made rich in every way so that you can be generous on every occasion, and through us your generosity will result in thanksgiving to God. This service that you perform is not only supplying the needs of God's people but it is also overflowing in many expressions of thanks to God. Because of the service by which you have proved yourselves, men will praise God for the obedience that accompanies your confession of the gospel of Christ."

We are blessed as we share with others. We live a happier and a more joyful life when we are generous with our possessions that we are able to give to others according to our ability. The Dictionary tells us that the meaning of caring includes feelings of loving kindness, looking after others, and providing food. To share means a sense of responsibility, a willingness to reveal that we care. To be generous is to give freely, volunteer our assistance, time and talents, and to give without expectation of return or reward. God blesses a cheerful giver.

Dear Lord, help us to care and share generously as we are able. Lead us to our neighbour who may be in need. Amen.
*NIV

Openhearted

"Just look what I received in the mail," my husband told me. "I am rich!" My husband retired forty years ago when he sold his Grocery Store in the northern area of the province. He never denied groceries to farmers who didn't have cash available at the time of their purchase. His willingness to help others led him on rare occasions to drive first nation people home with their groceries. He left the store unattended at such rare times. "I usually made money when no one was available to give them change." He was awakened in the late night hours by hearing someone filling their truck with gas from his pump. "I went back to sleep. I knew this fellow would be back to pay for the gas." He came back, paying his bill the next morning. However, not all farmers paid their store keeper the money they owed him at the time of his retirement. Hence the arrival of a generous check in the mail forty years later came as a pleasant surprise. A son, an executor of his father's will, discovered the unpaid bills. This gift touched the spirit of the "openhearted" retired store keeper. He was rich; rewarded with appreciation for the son who paid his father's debt.

My husband was a positive source in the community. His example of living an honest and faithful life as the local store keeper endeared people to him. He inspired others to do their part in showing help and support to every member of the community they encountered each day.

We read in Hebrews 6:10-11*, "God is not unjust; he will not forget your work and the love you have shown him as you have helped his people and continue to help them. We want each of you to show this same diligence to the very end, in order to make your hope sure." We will serve others!

Dear Lord, may we show love and concern for our neighbour as You shower Your blessings on us. Amen.
*NIV

Seventy Four

A Storm in My Life

"I have Parkinson's Disease," announced my husband after a visit to his Physician. Married life had brought renewed joy to a widow and a widower. Finding love again for two lonely people rekindled deep happiness. But the loss of smell, loss of taste, unsteady gait, and a shuffling walk were Parkinson's symptoms that could not be missed. The accordion remained on the shelf in the closet. The organ keys were untouched. The intensity of the disease increased. Life continued at a slower pace. At no time did my husband complain. "I do not have pain" was his comfort and consolation; a characteristic comment made by a man who always looked for the positive aspect of any situation he met in life. The Home Care visits brought sunshine to breakup the normality of each day.

The day came when complications of Parkinson's Disease took the life of my beloved husband. The storm that hit me was piercing and painful. I am at a loss to describe adequately the raw tearing away of part of my inner being. I wondered how people cope at such a loss as mine when they do not have faith in a loving Savior. Only Christ can bring comfort and eventually peace in times of sorrow. I was touched when our Physician told me, "Some day you will meet again."

All of us will sometime meet storms in our life. We do not understand why, but one thing we do know is that God walks with us all the way. God, in heaven above, sees our sorrow and hears our prayers. 11 Corinthians 1:3* tells us, "Praise be to the God and Father of our lord Jesus Christ, the Father of compassion and the God of all comfort, who comforts us in all our trouble so that we can comfort those in any trouble with the comfort we ourselves have received from God."

Dear Lord, thank you for your love and comfort. You are my rock and salvation. Amen.
*NIV

Seventy Five

Blessings

The gift of a second marriage brought happiness beyond measure. Not only did I receive the joy of love again in my life, I also received the gift of a step family that enhances my days. My children, though now adults, were blessed with a step father. His loving behavior with grace, and compassion endeared himself quickly to them. My family was happy for me. They rejoiced that their mother was not alone. They rejoiced also that they again had a father figure in our family.

I am appreciative of my step family. I can never replace their biological Mother and Grandmother but I did love their late Father. I love the family that my husband dearly loved. I wish to carry on that love to the best of my ability. I have experienced joy in knowing that I have been accepted as a member of their family. I proudly carry on the name my husband gave me.

I visited a former teacher in Long Term Care who had reached one hundred and three years old. I did not expect him to know me. I was surprised to hear him say, "Here comes the lady who has changed her name twice." Yes, I did and I rejoice for the many blessings that it brought me.

We can be thankful to God for His mercies He bestows upon us even if we have reached our so called "Golden Years." Proverbs 16:31* tells us, "Gray hair is a crown of splendour, it is attained by a righteous life." We elders are blessed, despite our age, with the gift of love, of belonging, and of joy. Joel 2:28-29b* states, "I will pour out my Spirit on all people. Your sons and daughters will prophesy, your old men will dream dreams, your young men will see visions - I will pour our my Spirit in those days." God is good. We are blessed.

Dear Lord, thank you for the many blessings you bestow upon us from childhood to old age. Amen.
*NIV

Seventy Six

The Good Samaritan

"I was stranded on a strange road," a new resident of our city told me. "I took a shortcut road that I had heard would lead me to our farm that was some distance from our hometown." She went on to say, "I suddenly realized the truck had a flat tire. I didn't have a phone so I could not contact anyone." She paused briefly and then continued, "I had no idea how to change a tire." The unfamiliarity of the area added to the distraught dismay of her situation. She told me she was finally so relieved to see a truck drive towards her. "A gentleman stopped and asked me if I needed any help." She told me that he changed the truck's tire, and refused to take any payment for his deed. She went on to say, "I have been waiting to meet you because that kind man was your late husband." I was not surprised to learn that my husband had helped someone in need. That was his nature – to do good when a need arose. The fact that I had never been told of this gesture was also not a surprise. He never looked for any praise. He just wanted to be of service for anyone that was in need when it was within his power to do so.

I am reminded of a verse in Galatians 6:9a* "Let us not become weary in doing good." God knows and sees our hearts even if no recognition is offered. He blesses our motives of wanting to help someone who is in distress. We are to be compassionate in all situations. We need to show the same love that Jesus showed us when He died on the cross to pay for our sins in order that we may have eternal life in Him. We show a love for Christ when we show a love for others.

Lord, lead us to where we can be of help in Your service. Amen.
*NIV

Seventy Seven

My Miracles

The phone rang sharply, interrupting a leisurely breakfast. "This is your Ophthalmologist's office calling. We have received a cornea for you. Be at the hospital at 9AM tomorrow." I had waited for over two years for this call. My sight had gradually diminished. The phone book, news paper, and price tags at the local store were my adversaries. I wept when told, "Your eye sight no longer qualifies you to be eligible for a driver's license." Fuchs' Dystrophy, I was told, is a slowly progressive deterioration of the cornea, the dome-like window that covers the front of the eye that allows light to pass through to the retina which enables me to see. "Dear God, "I often prayed, "I do not know how I could ever cope in a dark world. Please do not let me go blind."

God performed a miracle for me. He enabled the skilful hands of my Ophthalmologist to replace my defective cornea with a viable one. My world was no longer cloudy and blurred. But someone had to die before I could receive this gift of restored sight. I will forever be grateful to my cornea donor. I will never meet this person who left a legacy of love and caring for others by example. A compassionate person made a decision to donate a priceless donation. I was the recipient of this gift, too valuable to price in monetary terms. I later received a second transplant. I had a driver's licence again. I was blessed.

Scripture tells us Jesus performed many miracles. But do we believe Jesus performs miracles today? Do we ask God in faith, never doubting, when we have urgent needs? Have we come to expect the ordinary from the world around us? Our Savior waits for us to bring our requests to Him. "Look to me and answer, O Lord my God. Give light to my eyes." Psalm 13:3a*.

Dear God, teach us to wait with expectant hearts when we bring our needs and concerns to you. Amen.
*NIV

Seventy Eight

Obedience For Our Own Good

$\mathcal{O}$ur world has experienced a pandemic. COVID 19 is a disease universally prevalent that has hit many regardless of age, race, and social rank. Many patients who have recovered from this illness tell of painful experiences, and fear lasting effects. But most alarming are the thousands of people who have succumbed to this vicious virus. However, there are individuals who oppose Government control measures, as wearing masks, social distancing, restrictions to travel, and various services advocated to protect others and ourselves.

We are a social people. It may not be easy for part of our population to remain at home, out of community circulation. Only essential shopping is done. Our world has become smaller.

We do not compare Moses, one of God's greatest of prophets, to our Governing leaders today. However, have we, as human beings, now changed in our reaction to authority, sincere and for our own good as it may be? Are we willing to forgo our own limited knowledge, and take direction from professionals who have the expertise to help protect us from this illness, and possible death?

Acts tells us that God chose Moses to free the Israelis from bondage in Egypt. They had seen miracles in Egypt, and knew God had defeated the Egyptian armies at the Red Sea, but they grumbled for forty years. Scripture leads us to believe one of Moses' most remarkable characteristics was his concern for the Hebrews, in spite of their rebellious ways. Did they not have any vision to how good things could be? Was not Moses's leadership, directed by God, to lead the Israelis to a life of victory? They resented authority. Do we do the same today?

"It was this Moses whom they rejected when they said, 'Who made you a ruler and a judge?' He was sent to be their ruler and deliverer by God himself, through the angel who appeared to him in the bush." Acts 7:35*.

Dear Lord, help us to live in victory, without grumbling, obedient to your leading. Amen.
*NIV

Seventy Nine

God Remembers.

"I'm lonely, God," I prayed as I sat in the local Heath Unit Clinic Waiting room. "All these couples coming through the door have each other and I am sitting here alone." I had waited patiently for the time I would be able to get my COVID 19 vaccine shot. Watching people, when it is not obvious to others, quickly passed the time for me. A caring husband supporting the faltering steps of his spouse, a wife pushing her handicapped husband in a wheel chair, and another couple who appeared to be far too young for the age group now allowed, brought a piercing longing within me for the husband that was no longer at my side.

I immediately fell asleep when I retired early that evening. I, somehow, in an unexplained way, became conscious of my husband looking down at me. The comfort of his appearance overcame me with joy. My dream soon ended but as I awakened, an intense feeling of contentment filled me with peace. I was reminded of telling God about my loneliness at the Clinic earlier in the day. God remembered. He blessed me with the vivid presence of my husband if only for a few moments.

We can bring any concern or longing to our Creator be it of little significance or an alarming crises. We read in Psalm 38:9*, "All my longings lie open before you, O Lord; my sighing is not hidden from you." It is reassuring to know that God waits to hear from us. We can leave our every care at His feet, day or night. Why do we sometimes fear nightfall? God can come to us with the gift of comfort in the darkness of the night. The Psalmist tells us in Psalms 119:55a* "In the night I remember your name, O Lord." We are blessed.

Dear Lord, thank you for remembering my sighs of longing; remembering my loneliness in the day and in the night. Thank you for your constant comfort and peace. Amen.
*NIV

Eighty

I Press On!

The year was 1970. My husband was recovering from his second heart attack. He requested me to locate a document from his desk in the Pastor's Study in the church. I was rummaging through his desk drawer when I came across an envelope that unnerved me markedly. "To be opened in the event of my death" was written across the sealed envelope. There were further times when I was asked to fetch articles from the office. The threatening envelope startled me on each occasion. However, I was soon to learn the contents of envelope gave me all the information and guidance that I needed at the time it was required.

Thank you for walking with me through these pages, non threatening pages, but pages filled with the gift of life that has been given me these ninety three years. You, no doubt, have met experiences that have differed greatly from mine. You have walked down different paths that have influenced your life, shaped you, and brought you joys as well as sorrows. This is life. I pray that you might be blessed as I have been knowing that God walks with us each day of our lives.

My High School Graduation class at the Saskatchewan Lutheran Bible Institute in Saskatchewan --years ago for me – chose Philippians 3:13b-14* as our motto, "But one thing I do: forgetting what is behind me and straining toward what is ahead, I press on to the goal to win the prize for which God has called me heavenward in Christ Jesus." I am forgiven! I pray for a life of faith as I walk on with God.

I was shocked, as I was typing this last page of my "Legacy" to have my faithful computer crash. I am concluding this page using my new computer. I received a fee reduction because "I will soon be running out of gas." Gas in my tank or not, I will press on as I walk with Christ. Thank you for remaining at my side!
*NIV

Biography – Sylvia Engen Espe

Sylvia Engen Espe, retired from a career in Health Care, lives in Camrose, Alberta. She is an author who has varied interests in life. She enjoys photography, handwork, and travelling as well as writing. Her freelance involvement began in the early teen years, and actively continues to this day. Her previous book, "A Celebration of a Century," was published a few years ago. She has had numerous articles, including award winning articles, published in various periodicals. Her non-fiction writing has been an inspiration to many. But the pride and devotion of this ninety-three years old is devoted toward her children, grand children and great grandchildren. Relatives and friends cannot be excluded!

CPSIA information can be obtained
at www.ICGtesting.com
Printed in the USA
BVHW031929250921
617529BV00001B/2

9 780228 860105